CHARISMATIC GIFTS

CHARISMATIC GIFTS

By
KURT E. KOCH, Th.D.

THE ASSOCIATION FOR
CHRISTIAN EVANGELISM (QUEBEC) INC.
747 81st Avenue
Chomedey, Lavel (Montreal)
Quebec, Canada

ISBN 0-88981-000-1

First Edition 1975

Printed in the United States of America

CONTENTS

HASTENING TO THE END

From the movie world

During the spring of 1974, while I was in the course of my thirty-second lecture tour in the United States, the motion picture *The Exorcist* was playing in the cities. Wherever I went, the clergy not only asked me what I thought of it, but they organized meetings in their churches for me to speak about the problem of exorcism.

The founder and director of the radio program "Youthtime," John DeBrine, rented a large hall in Boston, big enough to hold twenty-five hundred, and invited young people to hear my discussion of *The Exorcist*. To our great surprise, more than two thousand young people attended.

What was the reason for this unusual popularity?

At the very time I was lecturing in Boston, this ghastly film was playing. Every day thousands would stand in line, often for several hours, in order to get tickets.

Let me say at once that I did not see this picture, although I was invited to go. Christians must not expose themselves to this demonic atmosphere. Billy Graham also issued a public warning about going to see this picture.

My knowledge of the film derives from a psychiatrist who went three times to see the film that had brought him so many new patients.

Why do I speak of a demonic atmosphere when discussing this film?

The Exorcist is based on a book with the same title by Blatty. The author is a Catholic and was brought up in a school run by Jesuits. Blatty is also a spiritist. Two of the major roles are played by actual Jesuits, Blatty's former schoolmates.

Both the book and the film are about a mysterious illness that afflicts Regan MacNeil, a twelve-year-old girl. When she is present, heavy pieces of furniture move without visible cause. A priest is summoned to the haunted house, but he cannot subdue the girl. He is thrown through a window by her. A psychiatrist is also helpless. Everyone who comes to see the possessed girl is not only subjected to verbal abuse but spat upon with foul green slime. She invites everyone present, even her own parents, to have intimate relations with her.

When all possibilities of helping the psychic or possessed girl are exhausted, a priest is sought out who is experienced in exorcism.

The priest takes up the cause of twelve-year-old Regan. He commands Satan to show himself. The duel is so taxing for the father that he suffers a heart attack. A younger priest takes over. He challenges Satan to leave the girl and take his own soul in return. Satan apparently agrees to this exchange, for the priest jumps out a window and dies a suicide. In this manner the tormented girl is cured.

This conclusion to the terrible spiritual campaign is as unbiblical as the whole story. No Christian can give his own soul as a sacrifice for another's life. Such a sacrifice is possible only through the death of Jesus on the cross.

Quite apart from the unbiblical incidents, this motion picture is crammed with such blasphemies and obscenities that merely watching it makes the viewer guilty in the eyes of God.

The film's effects on audiences reveal its demonic nature. At each showing in the United States, an average of four to six viewers faint. Many vomit. Pregnant women suddenly go into labor and have a premature delivery. Sensitive people suffer a nervous breakdown or become delirious.

I have at my disposal the firsthand reports of eyewitnesses. In Minneapolis I was the guest of a policeman who is a Christian. He invited to our discussion a colleague who had been on duty at this theatre. He had been obliged to bring delirious youths to the hospital in an ambulance. The victims of the film were not in a normal state of consciousness. The doctors injected sedatives, but they were totally ineffective.

We find here an interesting phenomenon, which I have already described several times in my books. In the case of mediumistic psychoses, mediums, and people possessed by demons, narcotics do not help. This fact helps distinguish these afflictions from mental illnesses.

But this is far from describing all the effects of this satanic film. Normally all those who take part in the production of such films come to grief. During the course of filming, one accident followed another. In one period of ten days, three of the participants met with death. The actor who was thrown out of the window actually fell dead a week later. The daughter of another actor was run over by a motorcycle on a deserted stretch of road. Some of the sets burned down. An actress had several nervous breakdowns.

"America is under attack by Satan in person," wrote one popular magazine. This statement hits the bull's-eye. In the United States one horror film follows another.

Just think of Roman Polanski's gruesome pot-boiler, *Rosemary's Baby*. A girl is supposed to have become impregnated by Satan. In other words, it is the age-old problem of incubi and succubi which I discussed from the perspective of pastoral theology in my book *Christian Counselling and Occultism*. This director Polanski also had to suffer the consequences. His pregnant wife Sharon Tate was slain along with other friends by the satanist Charles Manson. Anyone who makes such films is pursued or "shot down" by demons.

The atrocious rock opera *Jesus Christ Superstar* is on the same level. Judas is glorified and Jesus is depicted as a weakling. An intimate relationship with Mary Magdalene is also imputed to the Son of God.

Such films and operas are the black messengers announcing the fall of Western civilization. Demons multiply everywhere. Judgment is not far off.

Just before this book went to press, I was informed that the German version of the film, *Exorzist*, was abbreviated. Pornographic and blasphemous sections were eliminated from the American version. I am nevertheless astounded that the film was labeled "worthwhile" by secular reviewers and even an ecclesiastical board.

Despite the censorship of the American edition of the film, the first sinister effects are beginning to appear in Germany. Near Kaiserslautern an American soldier took his own life after seeing the film. Dr. Michael Kirsch, the district attorney at Kaiserslautern, initiated court proceedings with the purpose of prohibiting the showing of this film in Germany.

From the *Salzgitter Zeitung* of November 23, 1974, I quote from the letters to the editor. These letters were written by Pastor Horst Joost and Dr. Werner Gitt. They include the following statement: "A new wave is advancing, the wave of exorcism, with its occult ceremonies and cult of Satan. Unfortunately, the film *The Exorcist* has also passed through our area, capsizing those who have viewed it. Many went to see the film, perhaps unsuspecting, and came away desperate, terrified, tormented by fears, so that in other cities many had to be sent for psychiatric help. Even worse cases have come to light. A young sailor was so overwhelmed by the film that he took his own life the very same night. A seventeen-year-old from the vicinity of Wolfsburg killed one of his friends after seeing the film. He explained this bloody deed by saying, 'I, too, have the Devil in my body.' "

A student of the Heidelberg University committed suicide having seen *The Exorcist*.

It was left to *Der Aufruf*, a church newspaper in Germany, edited by a liberal theologian, Dr. Sturmer, to declare this film inoffensive.

During the correction of the proofsheets of this book I received shocking information from Denmark. My reporter wrote that a blasphemous film is going to be produced with the title "The Sex Life of Jesus Christ". Originally a cultural institution had promised to give a contribution of $170,000. After strong opposition from Danish believers the offer was withdrawn.

All these demonic revelations of hell are a sign of the end time. The world situation has grown more terrible than the sins of Sodom and Gomorrah.

From the political arena

I have no political ax to grind. I view the course of events only from the perspective of the prophetic word of the Bible.

It seems as though the Second World War fired the starting pistol for the eschaton (closing events of the age) in the narrow sense.

The major feature is what is happening to Israel. Since I have already discussed this problem several times in other paperbacks, I will not repeat the argument here. The time of fulfillment for Israel has dawned, even though Israel itself remains unaware of this fact. The Arabs and Palestinians may plan their campaigns, arm themselves, and rage. Everything will come to pass as it is predicted in the prophetic word. Without knowing it, the enemies of Israel are the means by which prophecy will be fulfilled. Israel is the crisis of world politics.

World Communism is a militant ideological and political movement of the present day. It stands beyond the dividing line of Israel and seeks to rule the world.

World Communism has the best chance of winning the race to rule the world. It is in the best position.

Militarily, it is probably ahead of every other world power by several noses. While the United

States was squandering billions to land a man on the moon, Russia was developing sinister offensive weapons. Russia is more realistic.

It was the summer of 1973. From a high-ranking officer of a foreign country I learned the following details about Soviet arms. After the American reconnaissance plane U2 was shot down over Russia, the Americans called a halt to this kind of spying on Russia. But the Russians were even more cunning. They built a reconnaissance plane that spies on American territory from an altitude of twenty-three miles.

Another project where the Soviets are ahead of the Americans is the development of a ship-to-ship missile. What was still a military secret in 1973 was trumpeted to all the world by the media in 1974. The Russians can sink American ships by means of missiles at a range of two hundred to five hundred miles. The sinking of the Israeli warship *Eilath* by the Russians represented a successful trial of this weapon.

These ship-to-ship missiles fly toward their goal automatically. They are guided by radar, infrared detectors, or lasers. The ships under attack have only ten to thirty seconds for defense. This problem is not yet satisfactorily solved.

The military threat to the world posed by aggressive world Communism is not, however, the major problem. Ideological contamination and subversion is a much more effective path to world domination.

Year by year the mendacious ideas of world Communism find increasingly fertile soil. Catastrophic famines prepare the soil for glittering promises that are gladly believed but never fulfilled.

11

Where Communism gains control the poor become even poorer, and the rich have to hand over their abundance to the Red dictators.

The propagandists of the left have succeeded in making decisive inroads among the students. They cover the university buildings with Communist slogans and plot demonstrations in support of left-wing causes. The students of today are the leaders of tomorrow. We know what is in store for us.

Most tragic of all is the Communist subversion of the major church organizations, whether in Washington or Geneva or in the ecclesiastical press.

It has been shown that fifty-four pastors in West Germany have the handbook of the Communist Party. A pastor in Hesse delivered speeches in support of the Communists from his pulpit. When his congregation complained to the church authorities, there were lengthy arguments. Finally the consistory had to yield to congregational pressure. The Communist pastor was to be transferred to a hospital chaplaincy. He refused and was suspended. We should not be surprised at the "Red clergy" in Hesse. Niemöller, the former president of the church in Hesse, accepted the Order of Lenin and an honorary doctorate from a Communist university. Of course there are also students and clergy who are legitimate.

I had another experience at Rotenburg, Germany. One of my friends came to the theological seminary there and was amazed at the pictures of Mao on the walls of the theology students. My friend addressed these students: "How do you reconcile it with your faith and studies to admire pictures of a Red tyrant who closed all the Christian churches in Red

China?" The students replied: "World Communism will carry the day and be victorious. Why shouldn't we protect ourselves?"

All these experiences, repeated with variations throughout the Western world, are symptoms. Satan has taken the field for his final battle against the returning Lord. Consistently developed Marxism is a powerful weapon in his arsenal for his war against the saints of God.

Many will interpret this as a political statement. I will respond by delineating my position.

At the moment one of my friends is engaged in the study of Marx and his writings. This friend surprised me with an interesting letter. The path of Karl Marx went via Trier, Berlin, Bonn, and Paris to London. It was in the English metropolis that the crucial stamp was placed on Marx's personal life. In England he joined a Satan cult and sold himself to the devil, sealing the transaction with his own blood. Following this act, he declared: "It is my duty to drop mankind into hell. There I will laugh at them."

Please read Wurmbrand *Was Karl Marx a Satanist?* (Available from Jesus To The Communist World P.O. Box 11, Glendale, California 91209.)

Anyone willing to expend the effort to study the sources should take four years and go to the University Library at Heidelberg to read the eighty-three titles published by and about Karl Marx.

The fact is that today a third of mankind is ruled by the tenets of Marxism. Another third is under the influence of Marxist ideology.

At the risk of being boring, I will repeat that for me these are not political statements, but only the fulfillment of the prophetic words of the Bible. Reve-

13

lation 6 speaks of the red horseman who will paint our earth red not only ideologically but with the blood of the slain.

We are racing toward the end with giant steps. The actuality of the Bible, the spiritual gravity of the prophetic word, increases each year. Anyone who is not afflicted with spiritual blindness will find this obvious.

"The night is far spent, the day is at hand," says Paul (Rom. 13:12).

DISCERNING OF SPIRITS

The Revelation of the Apostle John is the book of the Bible that has the most to say about the events of the eschaton. One sign of the spiritual and religious development that precedes the return of Jesus is the maturation of good and evil. About this process, Revelation 22:11 states: "He which is filthy, let him be filthy still: . . . and he that is holy, let him be holy still."

We live in the century of revivals and pseudo-revivals. These awakenings, spiritual or not, are associated with the maturation just mentioned.

Revivals

The Lord is hastening forward with His people. That is the impression we get in the twentieth century.

14

On every continent the exalted Lord has set beacons to serve for the preparation of the children of God. We will mention a few.

From 1905 to 1908 God bestowed the wonderful revival in Wales. During the same period there began the Korean revival, whose influence is strongly felt even today.

In 1931 a spiritual awakening was bestowed in *Ruanda* (Africa), which many volunteer helpers and evangelists carried into the surrounding countries. It was a springtime of the Spirit such as the dark continent had never before experienced.

Let us hear a brief account of this revival.

Before the First World War, the Bethel mission had gained a foothold in Ruanda, especially under their talented missionary Ernst Johannsen. There were already eleven missionary stations in existence when the German missionaries were expelled on account of the events of the war. But missionary work did not cease with their expulsion; for when the devil closes doors, the Lord can throw open gates.

After the war—it was in 1920—two young English doctors set out to work as medical missionaries in Ruanda. Both were spiritual products of the Welsh revival, and their hearts were aflame for the missionary cause. Since the Belgian government at first refused to issue the doctors an entry permit for Ruanda, they settled in the Kigezi district of Uganda, just at the gates of Ruanda. They had to wait only two years for political events to open the way to Ruanda for them.

As children of the great Welsh revival, the

missionaries prayed from the very outset for a revival in the heart of Africa. Special prayer meetings and weeks of prayer were organized, but there was no visible fruit in the early years. The national magicians mounted counterattacks and interfered with the missionary work.

Eleven years later, in 1931, the first signs of an awakening made themselves felt. The awakening did not begin with a turning to Christ on the part of the Africans, who were living in drunkenness and fornication. No, judgment began with the house of God. The staff of the mission was seized with a spirit of repentance and remorse. They asked forgiveness of each other and of God. During the worship services of the mission they confessed publicly that they had been obstacles to the awakening through constant friction, ambition, and dissension.

This acknowledgment of sin of the part of the whites and their attitude of repentance had a contagious effect on the Africans. The best example along this line is the overcoming of all dissension in the hospital at Gahini. The attendants and all the auxiliary personnel were dissatisfied, living in a state of constant friction. The instigator was the chief attendant Yosiya. Since he would not listen to either the missionaries or the supervising doctors, he was brought together with a renowned man of God, to whom it was granted to bring this trouble-maker to Jesus.

Yosiya came back as a humble Christian, who now had to put up with much ridicule in turn on the part of his fellow workers. But he did not give in to temptation. His way of life was a living Bible. His witness was contagious. The whole African staff of the hospital was seized with a spirit of repentance and a hunger for the Word of God. They came together for prayer and Bible study.

With this miraculous event the hospital at Gahini became a focal point. A lay movement came into being that bore the awakening far beyond the borders of the country. Uganda and later Urundi became involved.

One such campaign must be mentioned. On Christmas Day, 1934, seventy laymen assembled with their families at Gahini. They included deacons, evangelists, and craftsmen. They decided to undertake a joint missionary expedition to Urundi. It was a magnificent and risky undertaking. With their wives, children, and baggage they set out on foot for Buhiga, sixty miles away; from there they set out once more for Matana, ninety miles away.

The people in every settlement they passed asked the great caravan, "Why this migration? What are your plans, what is your purpose?" Thus they had opportunity everywhere to bear witness to Christ.

This great enterprise was blessed by the Lord. At Buhiga, during the very first year after the arrival of these evangelists more than six hundred came to Sunday worship. "The work of the Lord prospered, and he added to it daily."

This awakening in Ruanda, Uganda, and Urundi illustrates a principle that is familiar from the Bible, and is coming into play particularly in our century. Jesus sent His disciples out in teams. Seen from the missionary perspective, the twentieth century is the divine era of teams of lay evangelists.

We can state the following: The Welsh revival of 1905 sent out teams. Such a team came to Ruanda in

17

the persons of the two medical missionaries, Dr. Sharp and Dr. Smith. Teams from Ruanda crossed into neighboring countries and finally even arrived in Indonesia. At a distance, the Indonesia revival was fertilized by the Ruanda revival.

The people from Ruanda and Uganda also came to the United States and to Europe. I myself have had leaders of this revival—including William Nagenda—as my personal guests. Later I worked with William Nagenda in conferences on the Pacific coast of California and at Oxford in England. Another time I accepted an invitation to participate in a conference of the Uganda people at Kampala, Uganda.

Almost simultaneously with the awakening in Ruanda and Uganda, the Lord bestowed a magnificent spiritual awakening among the Wallamo in *Ethiopia*. Between 1936 and 1941—that is, in the very midst of the war between Italy and Abyssinia—the number of Christians increased from forty-eight to more than ten thousand. And this happened during the period when the missionaries had been hounded from the country. I have recounted this event in my book on Ethiopia.

Following the sequence of historical events, we must now turn our attention to Europe. The revival in the *Hebrides*, northwest of Scotland, was limited to the Gaelic-speaking area. Two single women had prayed thirty years for a revival. It came in 1949. At first the young men were affected. Every week they spent two or even three nights at prayer in a barn. The local pastor at first considered them fanatics. The young people, however, prayed fervently for their shepherd until he confessed himself a sinner and offered his life to the Lord Jesus. Then the spirit of repentance seized the older men. Only afterward did the movement extend to the women and girls. Under the influence of this revival, conditions on the islands changed. The pubs were closed. Businesses offering worldly pleasures had scarcely any patronage.

The revival in the Hebrides experienced two spiritual waves: the first in 1949, the second in 1953. I had an exchange of correspondence with Duncan Campbell, the leading brother, because I wanted to visit the Hebrides. He advised me not to come, because it is impossible to get anywhere with English among the Gaelic-speaking population. I succeeded, however, in getting firsthand reports from Duncan Campbell's daughter. This woman is married to a pastor whose church invited me for a week of lectures.

Parallel to the Hebrides revival, another spiritual event took place on *Formosa*. A woman of the Tayal race, whom I was able to visit, found Christ. At the age of fifty-eight she began attending a Bible school. Upon completion of her studies, she returned to her people and went from house to house as an evangelist. After the war this faithful labor gave rise to a powerful church movement that continues to this day. The high point was reached when five thousand members of this warlike people, who had defied Christianity for centuries, were converted and baptized in a single year.

The twenty-five years from 1950 to 1975 represent a kind of divine exclamation point. One might almost speak of eruptions of the Spirit. The faithful to whom the global events are a present reality have been brought to breathtaking heights.

In *South India*, Father Daniel, the spiritual heir of Sadhu Sundar Singh, was granted revivals among criminals and academics, among the rich and the very poorest.

Revivals were bestowed three times upon *Asbury College* at Wilmore, Kentucky. It is as though the spirit of its founder was brooding over the development of this school. No, it is not a human spirit but rather the Holy Spirit who has gripped the students there with powerful movements three times in the course of a quarter century. I was able to experience this myself somewhat indirectly during my two visits there.

The Asbury teams had the same missionary effect as the African teams. They bore onward the torch of the gospel. One particular fruit of the work of these teams may be mentioned. St. Andrew's University, in the state of Michigan, with its two thousand students, was likewise inflamed with the fire of revival.

A well-known London theologian once said to me, "Whether a revival is real or not can be seen from the establishment of new congregations." I can go along with this verdict, but have to expand on it by saying that spiritually dead congregations are brought to life through repentance and new surrender to Jesus.

If we apply this criterion to the Asbury and St. Andrew's revival, its genuineness is proved.

Now we must mention another revival of recent years, about which we have only scanty information. In the lands living under the Communist terror, such as Red China, North Korea, and Russia and its satellites, there has developed in the past four or five years a mighty hunger for the Word of God and communion with other believers. At the risk of losing their freedom, in the face of torture and capital punishment, these persecuted Christians have been confessing their faith. Probably these martyr Christians will rank in eternity far above us comfortable Christians of the West. The Communist countries are experiencing a furtive and often secret revival, from one individual to another. The living Lord can be felt in the midst of these believers, afflicted and tormented with the hatred of hell.

Among the mightiest revivals must be counted the revival on Timor, in *Indonesia*, with its influence on other Indonesian islands. During the period from 1965 to 1969, this revival was almost apostolic in nature. Nearly all the miracles familiar from the Acts of the Apostles were granted there afresh. These revival congregations, too, are today sending teams into every continent. Believers throughout the world are sharing in the blessing that the Lord has given there. The period of miracles gradually came to an end when those who were illiterate learned to read the Bible. The development of faith based on miracles into faith based on the Word is always salutary. Of course this does not mean that prayers are not answered, that men no longer have religious experiences, or that miracles have wholly ceased. The *experience* of God is part of the Christian faith.

Chronologically the revival on the *Solomon Islands* comes next. The instrument used by God is Muri Thompson of New Zealand. After several years of correspondence, we met personally for the first time at the World Conference on Evangelism at Berlin.

Our next meeting was on the occasion of my lecture tour in New Zealand. The Lord had singled him out to set the Solomon Islands ablaze.

It was on Thursday, August 27, 1970. Muri and his team were in a bush church at Sifilo, a village on the east coast of Maleita, an island in the Solomon group east of New Guinea.

Nearly three thousand people were assembled. After proclaiming the Word, Muri called upon those present to pray in silence. A solemn silence descended upon the great throng.

Suddenly Muri heard a violent roaring in the air. He thought a sudden storm had come up, and raised his eyes in fear. But the leaves of the trees were not moving. It could not be a storm. The roaring grew to hurricane proportions. For a moment, the evangelist thought it might be a jet making an emergency landing. Once again he raised his eyes, afraid the crowd was in danger.

At this moment the huge congregation was powerfully moved. The people fell to the ground, bewailed their sins, did penance or confessed to those lying beside them.

Now the evangelist realized that the power of the Holy Spirit had come upon all of them.

This even marked the beginning of a miraculous revival on the Solomon Islands. The pastors, the missionaries, the elders—all were gripped by a wave of purification and repentance. Stolen goods were restored. Criminals gave themselves up to the police. Old enmities were reconciled and ended.

The revival was accompanied by demonstrations of the Lord's power. The chronically ill were healed.

One example will be cited. A man in the final stages of tuberculosis had been discharged by the clinic as being incurable. At home he spent most of his time in bed. There was nothing left of him but a bundle of misery. When he was gripped by the revival, he pulled himself together and visited the mission station. In obedience to James 5:14 ("Is any sick among you? let him call for the elders of the church"), he asked the missionaries to pray with him. His request was met. Immediately after the prayer he was healed. This story is well attested, because the missionaries are witnesses to it. The man who was healed is today a skillful craftsman who makes canoes.

Conditions on the islands changed during the period of the revival. In the schools, where the rebellious spirit of the students caused the teachers much trouble, a new spirit reigns. The students read the Bible together with their teachers and hold prayer meetings.

Muri Thompson remained some three months in the islands. Wherever he went, the fire of revival was ignited. Here, too, the team system proved its worth.

One team under the leadership of Samson Sumbananga visited an infamous mining town, Bougainville. Through his friendly demeanor he won the hearts of the miners, who had been greedy for money and diamonds. Here, too, the Lord ignited a fire.

The Solomon Islands are the missionary field of the Australian South Sea Mission, part of whose territory I visited in 1963.

Next chronologically comes the *Canadian revival*, which began in Saskatoon during October of 1971. The first church affected was the Ebenezer Baptist Church of my friend Bill McLeod. The spark ignited many churches in many cities all over Canada. Bill soon asked to be relieved of his pastoral duties, and today he travels as an evangelist throughout Canada and the United States.

Among the most recent revivals is the spiritual awakening in *Thailand*. It was more than ten years ago that I traveled through Thailand with Rev. Pretel, the Marburg missionary. I became familiar with the stations and missionaries of the Marburg Mission: brothers Riemer, Klippel, Schuster, and Gagsteiger, as well as several pastors of the Thai church, whom I met at the invitation of Bishop Charoon Waichudist.

Ever since this visit to the Marburg stations I have prayed for Thailand these many years. In 1969, I was astonished to learn when I was on Timor that there, too, they were praying for the Thais. Petrus Octavianus has stood faithfully before the throne of God on behalf of Thailand.

I therefore rejoice all the more that a revival has been bestowed in North Thailand among the stations of the Marburg Mission.

A report from the missionary Otto Klippel contains the following: "We preached conversion, rebirth, justification, and the return of Jesus. This is important for church members, too. But it displeased some of the leaders who considered the sweet and perilous slumber of the congregations sufficient. The experience of personal salvation was almost unknown.

"I stressed repeatedly that there is only one way: total surrender to God. When the office of evangelization was entrusted to me several years ago, I was given a totally free hand. We went from congregation to congregation with our teams. We preached Jesus Christ, the crucified Lord soon to return. And then the Holy Spirit did His work in the hearts of men. They became concerned for their own salvation. Elders of the congregations, pastors, and simple Christians came in great throngs and confessed their sins. Thieves, prostitutes, drunkards, white-slavers, murderers and other such found forgiveness for their sins and salvation in Jesus. Entire congregations were transformed in the course of a few days.

"Prodigies quite outside my experience took place. More than once I stood helpless while a hundred or more, great and small, knelt in the churches and confessed their sins in tears. Often God spoke so powerfully through His Word that we all thought we were standing before His judgment seat. The preaching was interrupted because the sinners could simply not endure it any longer. They had to confess. What scenes there were! What had previously appeared totally impossible is taking place everywhere. It is a miraculous period of blessing after a lengthy drought.

"The only one who can do such things is the living Jesus of Nazareth. Him will we preach, despite the leading liberal theologians in Germany like Bultmann, Zahrnt, Käsemann, and others. My heart overflows with thanks and praise, and I want to let you share a bit in what is happening here."

I am very grateful for this report, and rejoice that such a time of blessing has come for the work of the Marburg Mission in Thailand, which I value highly.

This concludes our brief tour of the revival sites of our century. Lack of space has prevented us from mentioning many minor revivals. We have deliberately refrained from mentioning other movements that have often erroneously been termed revivals.

What does the increase of these revivals in our century mean?

Let me use a metaphor. For years I have been traveling by air from one continent to another. Each time we make a night landing, there are a variety of lights around the airport. Two miles from the runway are the farthest landing beacons, which orient the airplane as it lands. The runway itself is flanked by two rows of blue or amber lights so the plane will keep on the runway.

What is this meant to signify? With these revivals the Lord has set up signals—signals of His return, beacons to orient His community.

Will we take our orientation from these beacons?

Here is not the place to expound on all the features of the revivals. They have been adequately presented in my books dealing with the subject. One point, however, must be kept in mind. The revivals brought confession of sins, purification, and acceptance of salvation through faith. The converted and reborn Christians wrestled and prayed to walk in the light and to be made ready for the Day of the Lord.

For my circle of friends, I will list here the titles of

my books on the various revivals. This will make it easier for me to respond to the many inquiries I receive, not all of which can receive individual answers.

The accounts of the revivals will be found as follows:

Korea:	*Victory through Persecution*
Formosa:	*The Wine of God* (part III)
Solomon Islands:	*The Wine of God* (part II)
Indonesia:	*Revival in Indonesia*
	The Wine of God
Asbury:	*World Without Chance*
Canada:	*Revival Fires in Canada*

All of these books are published or distributed by Kregel Publications, Box 2607, Grand Rapids, Michigan 49501.

The Holy Spirit and alien spirits

The late Friedrich Heitmüller, the head of the Holstenwall congregation in Hamburg, coined the term "hybrid spirits." This expression can be taken in two ways, one wrong and the other right. It would be wrong to suppose that the Holy Spirit could dwell together with demonic spirits in a man. That is impossible. And Heitmüller did not mean it that way.

This expression means rather that alien spirits, frequently from the very lowest depths, give themselves out to be the Holy Spirit. Here we encounter once more the words of Scripture in II Corinthians 11:14: "Satan himself is transformed into an angel of light."

There are classic examples of how unholy spirits

can turn up in biblical disguise and lead men astray. I will mention a few.

Among those whose language is German, the books of Jakob Lorber (1800-1864) have spread much confusion. Lorber, a native of Austria, was not only a mystic but also a spiritualist medium. He wrote the so-called *Great Gospel of John* and *The Sun of the Spirit*. In my pastoral work, I have become familiar with the devastating effects of this "devout spiritualist."

In the English-speaking world, the best known of these hybrid spirits is probably Harry Edwards. He, too, is a spiritualist medium. He wrote the book *Spiritual Healing*. Edwards speaks of heavenly guides, his angels, without whom he can do nothing. What is seductive about him is the way he cloaks his demonic effects in a robe of Christian piety, so that even many Christians and Anglican clergy go to him for advice and assistance.

In America, Edward Cayce deserves mention. In his theories he resembles Jakob Lorber. Like Lorber, for example, he espouses reincarnation and asserts, like Lorber, that his powers and spiritual insights are of divine origin.

In the French-speaking world, I will single out a Catholic book that is presently receiving great attention and publicity among devout Catholics. I must here discuss this book briefly, although this means that I must disillusion my Catholic friends. The book is entitled *The Message of Gracious Love Addressed to Lowly Souls*. The author is known only by her given name, Marguerite.

Within the compass of its five hundred pages, the book contains, alongside some promising statements, a wealth of fantastic notions, if not out-and-out devout spiritualism. The contents consists of more than a thousand conversations between Jesus or His mother Mary and Marguerite. Devout Catholics actually believe that in these pages Jesus is speaking directly to Marguerite.

It is easy to demonstrate the contrary. We read, for example, on page 51 that Jesus entrusts Marguerite with the following commission: ''I wish for a world-wide day of prayer and worship, in reparation for sins and for the peace of the world.''

Of course I am in full agreement with a world-wide day of prayer for peace. But in speaking of reparation for sins this book is nineteen hundred years too late. The Epistle to the Hebrews says: ''For by one offering he hath perfected for ever them that are sanctified'' (10:14). Reparation for our sins was made long ago on the cross on Golgotha. If it had been Jesus speaking to Marguerite in 1963, He would have been declaring that His work of redemption on the cross was unfinished by ordering that there be days of prayer for this purpose today. It would have meant that the atonement on the cross for our sins was not total. It was not Jesus who spoke to Marguerite. It was a different spirit.

Another totally unbiblical statement is found on page 36 of the introduction to the book. Marguerite writes: ''What martyrdom Father had to suffer. And he loved Jesus so much. I think he had taken it upon himself to take away all my sins.''

The priest take away Marguerite's sins? That was done by Jesus. No human being can add to what Jesus did. Jesus said, ''What can a man give to redeem his soul?'' There is no such thing as vicarious suffering to take away one's own sins or the sins of others. To hold that there is, is a Catholic heresy.

In the case of these four figures from the realm of Christianity, we are dealing with hybrid spirits. But this means nothing more than that a demonic repast—or, in the case of the French book, religious naiveté—is being served up to the gullible under the guise of religious nourishment. All this has nothing to do with the Holy Spirit. The Holy Spirit does not mix. Only the devil stirs up confusion.

Much more complex is the problem of the hybrid spirit in the movement of the so-called Jesus People. This movement began in 1967 in Los Angeles. Let us take up this topic briefly.

In the course of my many trips in the United States, I came in contact, broadly speaking, with four parties among the Jesus People. Of course there are also many intermediate movements and splinter groups.

1. There is a satanic party, most visible in the "Prophets of Doom". They simply call themselves "children of God" and have gained much sympathy through the use of this biblical term. Their leader claims to be God and demands unconditional obedience. His followers live in strictly supervised communes.

2. There is a pathological group. Anyone who has ruined his nervous system with narcotics is open to all extreme movements.

3. The fanatical Jesus People are products of the

extreme pentecostal groups. They confuse a frenzied psyche with the Holy Spirit.

4. And there are certain young people who have experienced a clear biblical conversion in the Jesus movement.

Let us note at the outset that the movement of the Jesus People is already on the wane. Those who remain are the young people who were truly reborn, who found Jesus in this movement but then realized that they could not remain associated with groups devoted to hybrid spirits.

Anyone who takes a vertical cross section of the spiritual structure of the Jesus People will discover three strata. There are avowedly demonic young people who nevertheless bandy about the words and ideas of the Bible. Among them are the supporters of *Jesus Christ Superstar*.

Then there are those who use religious drugs to drive their minds into a religious frenzy. This, too, is not a genuine revival, but fanaticism.

Those that are left make up the small bank of people who have really encountered Jesus.

Taken as a whole, the Jesus People movement is the product of a hybrid spirit. In the case of individuals, however, there is no hybrid. A young person is either demonically inspired or led astray by his own unconscious—or filled with the Holy Spirit.

In any case, it is very difficult to distinguish spirits at all times and in all places. Often one cannot distinguish the spirit that controls the person to whom he is talking.

In many cases, all that I could do was pray to the

Lord to preserve me from false judgments. What immeasurable damage one can do calling God's work of the devil and calling what is demonic biblical!

Which of the gifts of the Holy Spirit do we need most under these circumstances?

At this point I would like to mention the case of a former hippie. From drunkenness and fornication, from narcotic addiction and begging, Lee Bryant experienced a clear conversion to Jesus and a call to service as an evangelist. She has become a source of blessing to many young people with similar addictions. Her book became a best seller in Canada. But do not let it fall into the hands of older, legalistically inclined believers. It is a book for men of the world, intended to show them the way—a task it will perform. It is entitled *Come, Fill the Glass*.

The mosaic of the tongues movement

All truly biblical spiritual movements are accompanied by hostile raids. The attacks are often made by the official denominations with their cold orthodoxy. Again, the opposition may come from heretical fanatics with their frenzied psyches. Can a sound biblical path be found through this chaos of contradictory opinions?

Before I started this chapter, I received a letter from an old friend who wrote to me: "I hope you have given your manuscript to some of the brethren to read. So much confusion reigns."

In fact it is with much prayer and anguish that I write what follows. I know in advance that I am too gentle and compromising for some, too harsh and ruthless for others.

The twentieth century is a century of tumult. It bears the stamp not only of world wars and political radicalism, but of heretical movements alongside the great revivals. Modern theology, for example, must be included here. Rudolf Bultmann, still alive in his nineties, has been much honored and decorated for his services to this cause. All the while, in the opinion of believers, he has been carrying out the work of hell. The Bible provides the accompaniment in I Timothy 4:1: "In the latter times some shall depart from the faith, giving heed to seducing spirits, and doctrines of devils."

But spiritual and religious chaos is also the product of firebrands who overemphasize and overvalue a biblical truth. Not everything is the Holy Spirit that is so labeled. Not everything is revival that bears the name. In this area I will mention the book *As At The Beginning. The Twentieth Century Pentecostal Revival,* by Michael Harper. I cannot follow either the title or the content of this book.

Already the gulf is fixed. I find myself falling between two stools. I cannot endure either the arctic chill of the modernists or the tropical heat of the extremists. In all my years as a follower of Jesus I have been concerned to follow a sound biblical line, without surrendering anything of the Word of God. To add nothing, to take away nothing, as Revelation 22:18-19 puts it, has been my concern. Roy Hession, the well-known English man of God, called the two opposite camps the Jesus-minus and Jesus-plus Christians.

Some historical data should be noted before we

embark on our survey of the pentecostal movement.

The first wave of the pentecostal movement spread in 1899 from a small Bible college in Topeka, Kansas, where Rev. Parham and twelve students became convinced that even in the twentieth century believers should be able to speak in tongues to demonstrate their baptism in the Spirit. This spark jumped to Los Angeles, and from there ignited a fire (in 1900) that swept over every continent. A Scandinavian named Barrat brought the new movement to Norway. The evangelist E. Meyer fanned the flames in Hamburg, Kassel, and Grossalmerode in Germany.

The resultant disturbances and unspiritual excrescences occasioned the leaders of Gnadau League to issue the so-called Berlin Declaration on September 15, 1909.

The second wave of the pentecostal movement spread in 1959, once more beginning in Los Angeles. This new version was somewhat different. It did not lead to the disturbances produced by the first movement. In addition, this second wave was more sweeping in its effects. It affected not only the pentecostal sects, but almost all the denominations in the United States. Today the pentecostal movement is found on every continent.

The third wave began in 1967, once more in Los Angeles, in the form of the Jesus People movement already discussed.

A fourth variant is the use of the term "charismatic movement" instead of "pentecostal movement," which referred exclusively to speaking in tongues. This current term is more comprehensive, because the charismatic movement is concerned not only with speaking in tongues, but with faith healing, visions, prophecy, and all the other charismata or gifts of the Spirit.

When the heresy of demythologization is compared to the theology of the pentecostal communities, one must say that many children of God can be found in the pentecostal sects and the groups associated with them, whereas this is impossible in the camp of the modernists.

Having made these preliminary distinctions, let us embark on our tour of the world. On this tour, I am not following the dictates of geography. My great concern is to cite positive events first. The reports that follow are all my own personal accounts, not second hand.

Saigon (Vietnam). An American officer was seriously wounded in the Vietnamese conflict. He sensed that his end was near. He continued to pray earnestly for his loved ones at home. When his death-agony began, he suddenly began to pray in a language he did not know. While he was thus praying, he had such a sense of peace and refreshment in his soul that his body, too, gained new strength. This praying in a foreign tongue marked a turn for the better. He recovered and was able to return to the United States.

For the sake of the record it should be stated that this officer did not belong to a denomination in which glossolalia was practiced. He had never had such an experience before, nor did he have any afterwards.

A psychologist would explain this experience as a product of the subconscious. In marginal conditions such as delirium, narcosis, and death-agony, the subconscious can achieve direct expression. Even if psychology seeks to offer a rational explanation, the blessing conferred by the experience remains. God can use both natural and supernatural means to benefit men.

Personally, I consider this Saigon experience both positive and genuine.

Soe (Timor, Indonesia). This took place several years ago. I was staying for several weeks in Soe, the center of the revival. I shared my room with one of the brethren who had come from another island. Today he is the most famous Indonesian evangelist. A year ago he was elected to the East Asian section of the World Council of Churches and was a delegate to the Lausanne Conference. He asked me not to give his name.

While we were staying together, he told me that once, when he was on his knees at night, he suddenly found himself praying in another language, which he did not understand. Several months later he came to Thailand as an evangelist and was astonished to discover that he was hearing people speak the language in which he had prayed earlier.

Praying in a foreign language was a unique experience in his life. He does not belong to the Pentecostal Church, but has many friends in the Pentecostal Church of Java.

I have no doubts about the genuineness of this experience, since I know this man very well. I have been with him on Java, on Timor, in Switzerland, and in Germany. He has a sober faith.

Bern region (Switzerland). During recent years I have sent from my Bible Mission thousands of New Testaments and Bibles to many of the Indonesian islands. The revival has led to a hunger for the Word of God throughout the countryside. Amos prophesied about this hunger. He proclaimed God's decision (8:11): "Behold, the days come, saith the Lord God, that I will send a famine in the land, not a famine of bread, nor a thirst for water, but of hearing the words of the Lord."

When a believer from the canton of Bern (not from the city of the same name) read my book about Indonesia, he felt compelled to contribute six thousand Swiss francs for the work in Indonesia.

I did not know the religious affiliation of this believer, but was pleasantly surprised to hear he belonged in Thun either to a pentecostal church or to the affiliated group of the Assembly of God.

Such joy in sacrifice is no rarity among those whom the theologians look down on. Since he asks to remain anonymous, I will respect his wishes.

It has long been my experience that the children of God belonging to the pentecostal churches or related groups put their critics in the shade when it comes to faith and generosity.

Lugano (Switzerland). The activity of the Pentecostal Church in Lugano is on a similar plane. On the first Friday of each month they fast on behalf of the martyr Christians in the Communist countries. What they save by fasting; the members of this pentecostal group contribute to support the Christians persecuted by the Communists.

It would be gratifying if many churches would follow this example.

Naturally it is also appropriate to point out that this congregation has members who speak in tongues.

Dortmund (Germany). Let us stay for a moment in the German-speaking world. From time to time I have received a significant contribution for the Bible Mission from a prayer group in Dortmund. I did not know who the contributors were.

During a week when I was lecturing in Herborn, five times a car with five occupants arrived from Dortmund. It turned out that they were my anonymous friends. I was astounded at their loyalty. To make a round trip of 130 miles on each of five successive evenings, 650 miles in all, to attend a series of evangelistic addresses—that was a sacrifice!

How astonished I was, then, to learn at their last visit that they were members of an Ekklesia congregation. The Ekklesia congregations are a product of the work of Hermann Zeiss, with whom I was quite well acquainted personally, but whose theology and message I rejected. His approach was that of the extreme pentecostalists.

These people from Dortmund know my position, and nevertheless support my missionary work. When I am especially in need of intercessory prayer I usually write to various prayer groups, for example the group in Zürich led by Josi Kuhn, or this Dortmund group led by Heidi Röll. In the spring of 1974, when I faced a difficult crisis, the Dortmund group replied: "We spent a day in prayer and fasting for you." I here take this opportunity to thank these friends.

I am not willing to assume the risk of subjecting faithful children of God to theological criticism merely because, in my opinion, they may have fanatical tendencies.

In many of the Ekklesia congregations—not all of them—great store is set by speaking in tongues.

Lancaster (Pennsylvania). During the course of several lectures at the Bible college in Lancaster, in the discussion periods many students asked me about glossolalia. I explained my position and said that for me glossolalia could be of divine, human, or demonic origin. In other words, it could be a charisma, a training of the subconscious, or an outgrowth of demonic roots.

When the discussion closed, the president of the college said that he could not agree with me at all points since he was of the opinion that the gifts of the Spirit came to an end with the definition of the New Testament canon.

The position taken by this scholar is that of so-called dispensational theology. The representatives of this theological party, which is widespread in the United States and Canada, believe that the gifts of the Spirit came to an end when the literature of the primitive Christian community was defined as the canon of the New Testament at the synods of Jamnia and Joppa (A.D. 201).

There is a kernel of truth in this theology. The Bible speaks of various epochs of revelation. The periods of Noah, Abraham, Moses, the kings, the prophets down to John the Baptist—all exhibit special features in the revelation of God. In similar fashion, the apostolic era with its charismatic activity is clearly distinct from the following epoch. There can be no objection to this analysis. It is only that I, along with thousands of believers, cannot accept the statement that the Holy Spirit shut up shop sometime in the course of the first two centuries. It is of the nature of the Holy Spirit that He is the representative of Christ in His church. The Paraclete, who brings the Word to life for us, who makes Christ a present reality for us, who distributes gifts and lends authority to the messengers of Jesus, and exercises His office from the outpouring of the Spirit on the first Pentecost to the return of Jesus.

Here, too, the members of the pentecostal churches can see I am not so far removed from them as they may think. In the course of my travels, pentecostal preachers have told me more than once that I have never experienced anything of the Holy Spirit.

For an introduction to dispensational theology, let me cite the book by the well-known British theologian E. W. Bullinger: *The Foundations of Dispensational Truth.*

Montreal (Canada). Now we come to the realm of glossolalia of a different kind. When I was giving a series of lectures in Montreal at the invitation of Gottfried Amend, on behalf of the Association of Christian Evangelism, three young men came to me for pastoral counseling. Their appearance was not promising. They had long hair and were dressed like hippies. All three arrived together. Despite outward appearances I had a sense of sincerity from the young people. They wanted to talk about glossolalia. All three acknowledged that they spoke in tongues.

I prayed inwardly for the guidance of the Holy Spirit. First we discussed the passages in the New Testament that discuss glossolalia. Then I passed to church history and the present era.

Finally I gave them the following advice: "Please pray as follows: 'Lord Jesus, if this gift of glossolalia is not from you, take it away. If it is from you, we want to use it for your glory.' " Then I prayed with my three visitors and said farewell to them. For a while I heard no more of them, since I returned to Germany.

Six months later I had an enormously joyful experience. All three wrote to me: "We have lost the gift of tongues. We have cut our hair. We are all attending a Bible college to prepare us to work as evangelists."

I have often advised people to pray for a decision from the Lord. I will now recount an opposite instance.

Los Angeles (California). I gave several lectures at the First Presbyterian Church of Hollywood. The next time I visited Los Angeles, I received an invitation from Rev. Blackstone. He informed me that a group of twenty-three who spoke in tongues threatened the unity of the congregation. They approached the other members of the congregation with the statement that only someone who had received the baptism in the Spirit was a full-fledged Christian. The gift of tongues was evidence of baptism in the Spirit. Rev. Blackstone asked me to help his congregation, because it had no idea how to deal with this group.

We agreed to attend a prayer meeting of these pentecostalists, provided that we would be admitted.

We agreed furthermore that we would pray in silence for a decision from the Lord as soon as the members of the group began to speak in tongues. Of the twenty-three, twenty-two usually spoke in tongues.

We came to the meeting. A young man belonging to Rev. Blackstone's own congregation welcomed him by asking, "Rev. Blackstone, when did you receive the baptism of the Holy Spirit?" This reception naturally had a strange effect. Rev. Blackstone is a devout Christian. After a brief introduction on the part of this young man, which was biblical but very brief, the meeting was opened for free prayer. A woman immediately began to pray in tongues. Blackstone and I at once prayed in our hearts, "Lord, if this gift is from you, bless this woman. If this gift is not from you, put an end to this group."

We awaited the decision of the Lord. It came. The speaking in tongues ceased. No one belonging to the group continued to pray, in tongues or in English. We considered that an answer.

Prayer deriving from the Spirit of God is never interrupted by the presence of two devout Christians.

Stuttgart (Germany). Petrus Oktavianus spoke in Stuttgart at my invitation. Since the crowd was enormous, the lecture had to be carried electronically to two additional rooms. There were about three thousand altogether in attendance.

After his address, Oktavianus called on the people to pray in silence. I was sitting with several others on the podium, because we had to make use of every last inch of space. During the silent prayer, one man on the podium suddenly began to pray in tongues. Once again, as in Los Angeles, I prayed for a decision from the Lord. Then I looked up to see how Oktavianus was reacting. He had himself prayed for clarity, as he later told me. There on the podium he turned to the man who was speaking in tongues and commanded him in the name of Jesus to be silent. And the trouble-maker fell silent.

Afterwards I asked Oktavianus, "Why did you command him to be silent?" He replied, "After I had prayed for clarity, it became clear to me that this speaking in tongues was not brought about by the Holy Spirit but by the enemy."

But I also spoke with the man who had been speaking in tongues, who came to me and apologized. He explained, "I didn't want to pray in tongues, but I was in the grip of force that made me do it."

"The spirits of the prophets are subject to the prophets," says Scripture (I Cor. 14:32). This man in Stuttgart was not master of the spirit who forced him to speak in tongues.

Even in Corinth, speaking in tongues had caused great dissension. Today the perplexity and uncertainty in this area are even greater.

Toyama (Japan). A most tragic event was recounted to me during my lecture tours in Japan.

43

Toyama is a Christian conference site on the west coast of Japan. The events to be described took place about fifteen years ago. The first harbingers of the second wave of the pentecostal movement in 1959 had reached Japan. Many Christians listened to them and found in their message the answer to their prayers for a revival. As a result, eighteen mission-aries from various missionary associations came to-gether at Toyama with the purpose of praying for a baptism in the Holy Spirit and the gift of tongues. It must be mentioned that these eighteen men were some of the best missionaries.

Day in and day out they fasted and prayed. And then it happened. They began to pray in tongues—at first a few individuals, then the whole group. This experience is simply called the Toyama incident.

The missionaries "baptized in the Spirit" re-turned to their congregations and preached: "Up to now, you have not yet had full salvation. You must receive baptism in the Holy Spirit and the gift of tongues."

The Japanese Christians did not submit to the new doctrine. They said to their missionaries: "You have been in Japan for more than ten years, and have never before preached full salvation to us. Who can say that you are doing so now?" This perplexity occasioned great confusion in these congregations. They broke apart. The congregations shrank. Fifteen of the missionaries left their calling and turned to another profession. Three of them recognized that they were on the wrong track. They renounced their pentecostal experience and stuck with their work. One of the three, whom I met and spoke with several years later at Karuizawa (Japan), took great pains to continue guiding his congregation. He died prematurely at the age of forty-six.

The Toyama incident was a spiritual catastrophe for missionary work. I have used this example several times to document my position. Members of pentecostal sects have replied by citing Luke 11:11-13: "If a son shall ask bread of any of you that is a father, will he give him a stone? or if he ask a fish, will he for a fish give him a serpent?"

Those who spoke in tongues interpreted this saying to mean: "We prayed that God would give us the gift of tongues, and so he does not give us a serpent."

There are two errors in this kind of biblical interpretation. In the first place, the Holy Spirit cannot be coerced and told what he is to do. Lukewarmness can grieve the Spirit, but so can legalistic coercion.

On the other hand, the Holy Spirit does not confess false doctrine. The theology of the pentecostal churches falls short at several points. The Holy Spirit confesses only the teaching of the Bible, not human invention. Therefore the response to "coercive" prayer can easily be a serpent instead of a fish.

A historical example can support this statement. In 1900, when news of the "glossolalia revival" came to Europe, the Norwegian evangelist Barrat went to Los Angeles. For thirty-nine days he spent several hours in prayer each day, praying for the gift of tongues. Finally he extended his praying to twelve hours without interruption. Then, finally, it came. Round about him people were falling down in ecstasy, as I experienced in Haiti. Barrat was infected by this spirit and began to pray in tongues. This "achievement" he then brought back to Scandinavia. From there this fanatical movement came to Germany.

Karuizawa (Japan). In Karuizawa I met a Lutheran pastor from California who tried to disturb our missionary conference. The whole story is too long to discuss here. During our meetings this Lutheran pastor organized parallel activities and drew away about forty missionaries.

Here we catch sight of a by-product of the pentecostal movement: dissension, schism, disorder. For this California pastor is a representative of the pentecostal movement.

When our missionaries returned, they reported: "The man from California spoke, sang, and prayed in tongues for an hour and a half. No interpreter was present. No one knew what he had actually said. After the meeting, one of our missionaries went to the pastor and asked him how to receive the gift of tongues. The Californian gave him the following instructions: 'Say a short prayer, like "Lord, help me," five to eight hundred times; then your tongue will be used to it and you will automatically begin to speak in tongues.'"

This is supposed to be the work of the Holy Spirit? It is a way of training the unconscious to produce glossolia on human terms. I even consider it blasphemy against the Holy Spirit.

Titusville (Florida). Invited by Rev. Peter Lord, I had some meetings in the wonderful Park Avenue Church. One of the assistant ministers informed me about a lighted sign in front of a church with the words: *We Teach Tongues Speaking*. And this will be a gift of the Holy Spirit? That is sheer blasphemy.

46

Stanwell Tops (New South Wales, Australia). At many theological seminaries and Bible colleges on every continent I have heard reports of the disturbances created by the pentecostals.

My friend Dr. Les Werry, leader of the Australian evangelistic movement Ambassadors for Christ, founded the Bible college at Stanwell Tops, which is now in Katoomba. The second wave of the pentecostal movement after 1960 also made inroads into his school. There were so many factions and so much dissension that the teachers could hardly work.

After much praying, Dr. Werry decided to take a radical step. He closed the school in the middle of the semester and told the students, "You can register for the next semester if you fill out a questionnaire." The questions were so worded that Dr. Werry could eliminate all those who were speaking in tongues. In this way the evil spirit was exorcised from the school.

Asbury (Kentucky). I was able to visit this college twice. The president told me that shortly after the beginning of the revival one of the pentecostal brethren appeared at the college and said to the students, "You are still lacking baptism in the Holy Spirit and therefore also the gift of tongues." He wanted to address the college, which the administration would not permit. Thereupon this pentecostalist insinuated himself into the dormitory rooms of the students, where he began to create havoc. The teachers in charge had their hands full getting rid of this interloper.

Saskatoon (Canada). In Saskatoon, the starting point of the Canadian revival, I stayed with Pastor

47

Philipp Grabke. When the evangelistic teams left Saskatoon for other cities, Mrs. Grabke joined one of the teams. When the revival came to Winnipeg, many pastoral assistants were needed. At this point a woman who spoke in tongues insinuated herself into the group of assistants without being appointed by the leaders. This hireling confused the newly converted with the demand: "Until you can speak in tongues, you have not received baptism in the Holy Spirit." When the leaders discovered this intriguer, they forbade her participation.

The attitude of the leading brethren of the Canadian revival is firmly opposed to the pentecostal movement. One pastor in whose church the revival had begun gave me on my visit a tape recording of a woman in Toccoa (Georgia) speaking in tongues.

At meetings of the prayer group to which she belonged, this woman constantly fell into glossolalia; there was no interpreter who could translate what she was saying. Finally the brethren asked her, "Pray in English—we don't have anyone to interpret." The woman did not do as she was bidden.

The brethren then determined to test this spirit. When the woman began to pray in tongues once more, they asked, "Thou spirit of tongues, dost thou confess that Jesus Christ came in the flesh?" No answer! The brethren repeated their question. Again the woman paid no attention. Finally the brethren spoke in command: "In the name of Jesus we command thee, thou spirit of tongues, tell us the truth: dost thou confess Jesus Christ?" Now followed a reaction that the brethren had hardly expected. From the woman issued a male voice, screaming: "No, I hate him." This made the situation clear. The woman's glossolalia was demonic.

This raised the question whether I should keep the recording in my house or destroy it. I gave it to a minister who had requested it.

St. Petersburg (Florida). One of the finest churches in Florida is the Northside Baptist Church, with a congregation of 2,500 members. Invited by Dr. Kenneth Moon, I had the privilege of teaching and preaching there. People came from long distances. Among them was a servant of the Lord who informed me about a strange experience with a tongues speaker. Because there was not an interpreter this counselor asked the tongues-speaking spirit: "Do you confess that Christ has come in the flesh?" (I John 4:2). First no answer. Finally the spirit replied: "I belong to a church."

"To which church?" asked the counselor.

"To the church of Satan," was the answer.

After this terrible confession the counselor commanded the evil spirit in the name of the Lord to leave the tongues-speaking woman.

Kalgoorlie (West Australia). North and northeast of Kalgoorlie lies the territory of the Wongai tribe. My informant is Peter Jamieson, whom everyone calls merely Peter the Black. He holds the rank of chief, but does not exercise it since he became a Christian and today works in New Zealand as an evangelist.

Peter told me that speaking in tongues had never been able to confuse him. The six magicians in his still heathen tribe all speak in tongues when they are in a spiritualistic trance. The first time Peter came across a man speaking in tongues in Sydney, he said, "That's nothing more than what we see our tribal magicians do."

Brisbane (Australia). My informant is Barbera Sganzerla, in whose house I was a guest. At the University of Brisbane the students asked me about glossolalia in the United States and Europe. I gave an account of it.

That evening at home Sister Sganzerla told me some experiences of the Assembly of God in Brisbane. A Greek immigrant joined this group, which is moderately pentecostal. Since he had not yet mastered English, during the prayer meeting he prayed in Greek, his native tongue. An interpreter jumped up and translated into English. The Greek responded, "I was not praying in tongues, but in my native language. The interpretation was wrong."

Following this unfortunate experience he joined another pentecostal group, where he experienced the same nonsense of having an "interpreter" misinterpret his prayer in Greek.

The Greek withdrew from this group, too, and tried again with a third. He was let down for a third time. Now this faithful Christian had had enough. He stated, "They're all liars." He thereupon joined another congregation where no one spoke in tongues.

Port au Prince (Haiti). My organizer Dean Hochstetler arranged a series of lectures for me in Haiti. He did not know what denomination the individual congregations belonged to. Despite this mishap, some good came of it.

Among other things, I was to address an International Conference on the Kingdom of God. At the very first meeting we noticed that we were facing preachers belonging to pentecostal sects and the Assemblies of God. They had come to Haiti from different countries.

The first lecture went quite well. I spoke about Luke 9:1-2, the threefold authority of Jesus' disciples. I was disturbed, however, by the prayer meeting that followed. The people ran around, clapping their hands. Some began to sing with a loud voice. Finally some sank to the floor and murmured incomprehensible words.

I almost reproached my organizer for bringing me to such a conference.

Things became worse with each lecture. Some pentecostal preachers leaped into the air while praying. Later I heard that they belonged to a group called the Jumping Church. They take Malachi 4:2 as their biblical authority: "Ye shall go forth, and grow up [RSV: leap] as calves of the stall."

During the third lecture, several women and young girls fell into a trance and spoke in tongues. But the pentecostal preachers also prayed in tongues. I have a clear memory of a well spread out American who was praying in tongues. After his prayer, he said, "Lord, give Thou the interpretation." Then he said in a voice that was at once supernatural and repellent, "I am the living God! I soon return! Be ready!"

A cold shudder went over my organizer and myself. We both prayed for God to protect us from this spirit. Dean said to me, "Please don't be angry. I cannot attend any more assemblies of this kind. Demonic forces are at work."

51

At the fourth lecture I did not have Dean with me. It was also my last lecture. I was interrupted in the middle by one of the preachers, who attacked me and shouted, "I doubt that you have received baptism in the Holy Spirit."

Only with great effort was I able to bring this fourth lecture to an end. I left the auditorium and went back to my hotel on foot.

That evening was the final assembly, which most of the participants attended. I did not have the strength to confront these spirits from the depths once more, and simply stayed away.

This was a valuable lesson for my organizer and myself. It was shown us once more how demonic powers can take the guise of the Holy Spirit.

Fortunately, the Lord in His mercy had compensation in store for us. A missionary society familiar with my books heard of my visit and issued an immediate invitation. With great haste the missionaries of the island were invited. Association with the missionaries restored my inward equilibrium.

I must now break off this mosaic picture of the tongues movement, although I have innumerable additional examples and experiences at my disposal.

I know what objections can be made to this compilation. The principle of negative selectivity can be cited. When every favorable example is omitted and only negative experiences are recounted, the picture that emerges is one-sided. That is not the case with this compilation. I have searched frantically for good examples. The negative experiences constitute an overwhelming majority.

The many excrescences are not themselves the deciding factor, but rather the deceitful spirit that sometimes controls entire congregations. I need mention only the Holy Rollers and the Jumping Christians.

The real problem, however, is not the extreme groups, but the moderate ones. In the case of the "wild" sects, anyone can see at once what is going on. In the case of the moderate groups, the question often arises of what verdict to pass.

For this reason I have been praying for years for the gift of discerning of spirits, and I beseech the Lord to protect me from false judgments.

At the conclusion of this painful but necessary chapter, I must once more say something positive.

Chicago (Illinois). The Moody Bible Institute had invited me to deliver several lectures. Some pastors belonging to the Assembly of God, a moderate pentecostal denomination, also took part. One of them immediately invited me to address his congregation. This was Rev. D.E., from Rock Island. I warned him by saying, "You know from my lectures that I have a negative attitude toward the tongues movement, although I recognize all the gifts of the Spirit." He replied, "I share your reservations. Our congregation needs your message." I accepted the invitation and delivered five lectures to this congregation, which was a congregation that gave me the impression of being thoroughly sober and biblically oriented.

Billings (Montana). Another pastor of the Assembly of God, Dr. Roger, also invited me. Here the spiritual situation was even clearer. It gave me great joy to speak before Dr. Roger's congregation. I would accept his invitation again.

It would therefore be wrong to lump all the pentecostal congregations or their related movements together indiscriminately.

After I had addressed several Assemblies of God in Canada, there came a series of invitations to the Caribbean Islands. I have already recounted my terrible experience in Haiti. A positive experience will be described in conclusion.

Trinidad (West Indies). An association of pastors of the Assemblies of God had invited me to visit San Fernando and its environs. These were Pastors Bagoutie, Persad, Foster, Krischna, Beam, and Sydney, among others. In their congregations I found no speaking in tongues at all. Neither did they espouse an unbiblical theology. I was delighted to hear that Joshua Daniel, the son of Father Daniel in Madras, had carried on evangelistic work in these congregations before me. He had laid a good foundation. In these congregations I found a genuine spiritual atmosphere.

At the conclusion of my work in Trinidad I spent some time with the pastor of a pentecostal congregation in Port of Spain. He said that, to the distress of the other pastors, no one in his congregation spoke in tongues. He put it this way: "Speaking in tongues is not a matter of primary importance to me. My children sometimes play 'church,' and have already hit on the idea of imitating glossolalia. They babble something incomprehensible." "My colleagues," he went on, "have already accused me of boycotting their work because I don't want to hear about speaking in tongues. They even want to exclude me from the Pentecostal Church. But I will not leave. I grew up in a pentecostal congregation and will remain in the Pentecostal Chruch even if I cannot accept much of what the other congregations do."

We parted friends. As we said farewell, he said, "If you ever come back to Port of Spain, please come to visit me and address my congregation."

Thus even in the pentecostal congregations there are pastors whose approach is biblical. I have spoken twenty-eight times before congregations of such pastors.

The first chapters of this book bring significant experiences to bear on the question of spiritual gifts.

The exalted Lord is taking pains to prepare His people. In no previous century have there been so many revivals in so many different places on earth.

The powers of darkness are likewise summoning all their forces for the final battle. They are casting a smoke screen over the battle lines. They are sowing confusion among the congregations. They are serving up a demonic repast disguised as true religion.

This chaos, this confusion requires a clear judgment and perception. More than ever, therefore, we need the gift of discerning of spirits.

EVALUATION OF SPIRITUAL GIFTS

A historical example will bring us to a proper understanding of the gifts of the Spirit.

During the Thirty Years' War, the small villages and isolated farms were often burned by the roving soldiery. The peasants tried to protect themselves. They built their houses behind hedgerows or beyond swamps and there cleared new fields. The access roads were cleverly camouflaged. They fortified the approaches, marked them with isolated birches or willows, and built dams so that the practicable roads were covered with six inches to a foot of water. Anyone going off the access road to the right or to the left would sink into the swamp and not be able to escape.

For me this has become a metaphor for the spiritual situation. Only one way is safe. Anyone diverging right or left will be swallowed up by trackless mire that will not support him.

The cold

When it comes to the gifts of the Spirit, this departure from the right way can be observed over and over again throughout church history and in the present age.

The official church constantly went off to the left. Hearts grew cold, the message of the gospel lost its force, the organization turned into a soulless machine. In my entire life I have never heard a pastor in the state church in Germany preach on the gifts of the Spirit. Of course such preaching probably took place somewhere. The fact that I have never run across it merely shows how rare it is.

Only once did I hear anything about this subject at the university; that was from my revered teacher Karl Heim. In his lectures on the Epistle to the Corinthians he naturally discussed the gifts of the Spirit.

What the church had too little of, the fanatical sects overvalued.

The genuine revival in Wales fell victim to the danger of becoming totally "spiritual." Its one great theme was the Holy Spirit, His operation and His gifts.

The hot

The pentecostal congregations of the present share this one-sidedness. This means, above all, the pentecostals of the southern countries, who allow themselves scandalous distortions of the biblical message. I am happy to note that there are some moderate groups as mentioned before.

A minor example of this theology that goes off the way to the right may be cited. The Dutch pentecostal evangelist Hoegendyk (the elder) was addressing the Bible college in Batu, on East Java. There he stated: "We need no longer speak of the cross and blood of Jesus, but only of the operation of the Holy Spirit."

The sound

Those who go astray to the left and to the right must be called back: "Be sound in faith!"

In I Corinthians 2:2, the apostle Paul says, "For I determined not to know any thing among you, save Jesus Christ, and him crucified." And what Jesus said must be taken to heart: "Ye shall receive power, after that the Holy Spirit is come upon you: and ye shall be witnesses unto *me*" (Acts 1:8).

At the Berlin Congress for World Evangelism, Billy Graham delivered the keynote address, emphasizing, "The message of the cross is the center of our preaching." Our preaching must be Christ-centered, not Spirit-centered. Christ must be the center, not the Holy Spirit!

That was also the watchword of Martin Luther. He said, "What promotes Christ is biblical."

The second thing we have to say to those who go astray to the left and to the right is, "We have the Word of God."

Holy Scripture came into being through the men of God who were inspired by the Holy Spirit and impelled by Him.

A few texts will be cited:

"The Spirit of the Lord spake by me, and his word was in my tongue" (II Sam. 23:2).

"I am full of power by the spirit of the Lord" (Mic. 3:8).

"This scripture must needs have been fulfilled, which the Holy Spirit by the mouth of David spake before" (Acts 1:16).

"Which things also we speak . . . in the words . . . which the Holy Spirit teacheth" (I Cor. 2:13).

"But the Comforter, which is the Holy Spirit, whom the Father will send in my name, he shall teach you all things, and bring all things to your remembrance, whatsoever I have said unto you" (John 14:26).

"Holy men of God spake as they were moved by the Holy Spirit" (II Peter 1:21).

The Holy Spirit has made Himself dependent on

the Word. Even His "free operation" must be tested by the Word.

Men of God in the present have always emphasized that the Holy Spirit is dependent on Scripture. Some will be cited.

"Even religious devotion can lead to sin, when it assumes itself superior to the Word of God," writes Hans Brandenburg in his commentary on Galatians (*Wuppertaler Studienbibel*, p. 67).

Dr. Fred Dickason, Dean of the theological faculty of the Moody Bible Institute, writes on page 3 of his booklet *The Spirit of Grace*: "The major role of the Holy Spirit is revealing the mind of God in the Bible."

Otto Rodenberg writes on page 90 of his book *Die Gemeinde Jesu Christi und die Bibel*: "The Holy Spirit who created Scripture linked himself intimately with Scripture."

Here I heartily recommend the booklet *Fromme Verführungen*, by Dr. Erich Lubahn. On page 12 he writes as follows: "The written word of the Bible provides the static side, which never changes; the Holy Spirit provides the dynamic side, the Word of God that gives, preserves, and supports life, encountering man. Both go together inseparably. The static without the dynamic leads to paralysis; the dynamic without the static leads to fanaticism."

These are words of great clarity and truth. Biblical sobriety is not a compromise but the necessary condition for a sound faith. To place too little or too great a value on something always leads men astray.

THE FRUITS OF
THE HOLY SPIRIT

Any evaluation of the gifts of the Spirit necessarily involves the question of the fruits of the Spirit. One might even venture to say that the fruits of the Spirit are more important for our faith than the gifts of the Spirit. We achieve more through what we are than through what we do. Our attitude speaks louder than our actions.

The life of Christians is the Bible of unbelievers. In the realm of the fruits of the Spirit there is much confusion. What matters is the initial impulse, the inward conditions of our life and actions.

Spurious fruits

A few years ago I delivered a week-long series of lectures at a church in West Essen. The pastor went on vacation so as not to have to listen to my lectures. (I was invited only by the elders.)

The pastor is in the modernist camp. His "gospel" is social activism. In one sermon, for instance, he stated that if it was up to him, the only people who would be baptized would be those who could produce a certificate of at least three months' social commitment. He meant that to be baptized a youth must work, say, for three months as a volunteer in a home for the aged or as a hospital attendant.

Of course such work is laudable. But it has nothing to do with the fruits of the Holy Spirit. The roots of such social activism are found in the person himself, not in Christ or in the Holy Spirit.

60

I experienced an even more extreme example in Brazil. I was visiting a home for vagrants in Porto Alegre. Following a tour of the institution, I had a serious conversation with the woman who ran it. I asked her what group the home was associated with. She replied, "We are spiritualists, followers of Kardec. We also have orphanages, old-age homes, hospitals, nursing homes, cultural centers, and schools." I was not a little surprised at such abundant social work on the part of these spiritualists. Therefore I inquired further: "What role does Christ play in your ventures?" My eyes grew even wider when she stated: "Jesus is our great example. He washed His disciples' feet. We also want to put His philanthropy into practice." Since I am only too familiar with spiritualism, I pressed the question: "Is Jesus not the Redeemer, the Savior, the Son of God for you and your friends?" "No," she replied, "He is only our example. He was a great man, who thought in social terms."

I do not want to be misunderstood. Naturally it is of great benefit for someone who is chronically ill to receive care in an institution. But this conversation points out the great difference in motivation. Two people may do the same thing, but it is not really the same thing. One acts out of a sense of social responsibility, the other out of love for Jesus and His neighbor.

Much fruit in Jesus

In John 15:5, the Lord says: "I am the vine, ye are the branches: He that abideth in me, and I in him, the same bringeth forth much fruit: for without me ye can do nothing."

Without me—nothing! That is what this saying of Jesus states. It is a radical, a terrifying saying! Without Jesus, volunteer work in the old-age home does no good. Without Jesus, our sacrifices of time and money are—nothing! Our heads cannot accept this harsh saying, which is as radical as the Sermon on the Mount. But Paul says something similar in I Corinthians 13:1, 3: "Though I speak with the tongues of men and of angels, and have not charity, I am become as sounding brass, or a tinkling cymbal. And though I bestow all my goods to feed the poor, and though I give my body to be burned, and have not charity, it profiteth me nothing."

Now from far off I hear contrary voices raised, saying to me, "Anyone who works as a volunteer in an old-age home demonstrates his charity and love by what he does." If he is a believing, reborn Christian, this statement is true. If not, however, he merely demonstrates his sense of social responsibility, his sympathy, his philanthropy. Jesus distinguishes the spirits. Only in Him is the fruit genuine. Only the fruit that comes through the operation of the Holy Spirit has eternal value. That is not my own opinion, but the statement of Holy Scripture.

We have heard it already in John 15:1-5, and hear it unequivocally in Galatians 5:22, 23: "But the fruit of the Spirit is love, joy, peace, longsuffering, gentleness, goodness, faith, meekness, temperance."

Exegetes have said, "The one divine fruit is love; the others are only reflections of this one."

Love is the first and highest fruit. It is both a fruit and a gift of the Holy Spirit. In Romans 5:5, Paul writes, "The love of God is shed abroad in our hearts by the Holy Spirit which is given unto us."

We must not overlook the fact that in the two passages where the apostle Paul speaks of the gifts of the Spirit, he ranks love first.

In Romans 12:6-8, Paul lists the gifts of the Spirit; immediately afterwards, in verses 9-10, he speaks of love.

In I Corinthians 12:31, the apostle exhorts the Corinthians: "Covet earnestly the best gifts: and yet show I unto you a more excellent way." Then follows the wonderful chapter on love and charity.

Transformation into His image

In the introduction to this chapter, I spoke of the inward conditions of our actions. This statement must now be elaborated on.

The program the Holy Spirit has for us is twofold. He incorporates us into the process of salvation, into the body of Jesus; then He continues the work that has been begun by transforming us into the image of Jesus. This statement can be clarified by two passages from the Bible. The first is Romans 6:4:

"Therefore we are buried with him by baptism into death: that like as Christ was raised up from the dead by the glory of the Father, even so we also should walk in newness of life."

In our conversion and rebirth, in our spiritual renewal, we are incorporated by the operation of the Holy Spirit into the reality of Jesus' death and resurrection.

Once we have been implanted, the Holy Spirit becomes holy restlessness within us, the architect whose goal is to transform us into the image of Jesus. In the second passage Paul describes this process as follows:

> "But we all, with open face beholding as in a glass the glory of the Lord, are changed into the same image from glory to glory, even as by the Spirit of the Lord." (II Cor. 3:18)

The twofold process by which the new creation takes place therefore consists of implantation and transformation.

I have met many who have experienced rebirth through baptism into the death of Jesus and have then reflected the nature of Jesus.

I am reminded of Otto Hecker, at whose table I sat every day for two years. He is the only one of the brethren in whom I did not find a single defect in the course of those two years. He was a father full of God's grace, faithful in prayer. I particularly recall one experience.

Otto Hecker, who has now dwelt with the Lord for several years, was by profession a master painter. One day an apprentice standing on the ladder accidentally tipped over a bucket of quicklime. Hecker, who was just passing by the foot of the ladder, had the whole bucket of lime dumped on his head. There was no outburst of anger, although he totally lost the sight of one eye and more that half the sight of the other in this accident. Naturally this greatly impaired his ability to practice his profession. He could hardly distinguish colors properly, though head of a painting firm.

I never heard a word of complaint of bitterness

escape his lips. Here we find I Corinthians 13:7 fulfilled: "[Charity] beareth all things, believeth all things, hopeth all things, endureth all things." He was a sanctified Christian.

I became familiar with another personal story while I was in Wuppertal. This one concerns Hanna Faust. Her friends called her simply Aunt Hanna. For forty years she had been married to a heavy drinker, who would often come home drunk and then torment and beat her in his rage. She never stood up to him, never reproached him, although he took all the money he had at his disposal to the bar while his household lacked even the bare necessities. At the bar he would make fun of his wife with his drinking companions, calling her a silly fool who took everything without complaining.

The more this drunkard tormented his wife, the more she cried out to the Lord for deliverance. One night, when he was once again really high, he made a bet with his companion: "I'll bet you ten glasses of beer that my wife will make us coffee without saying a word if we go home at three o'clock this morning and toss her out of bed." His friend replied, "That will be a good joke."

The two of them staggered home, where they woke up his wife by screaming and shouting. Without a word she got dressed. Praying silently, she made coffee for the two revelers and served them.

That was the moment when the Spirit of God was at work in the heart of her husband. The drunkard became sober. His face paled. He fell silent. When he had won the bet and his companion had left, he said in a different voice, "Wife, can you still forgive me? All this time you have been so good to me, and I have made life so hard for you."

They both knelt down. The drunkard surrendered his life to the Lord Jesus. He had been vanquished by the love of his silent but prayerful wife.

Here we see I Corinthians 13:4, 5 once more: "Charity suffereth long, and is kind; is not easily provoked, thinketh no evil."

When the fruits of the Spirit arise and develop in us, they show that we have been buried with Christ, have been raised with Christ, and walk with Christ in newness of life (Rom. 6:4).

Our moral qualities are never the source of the gifts of the Holy Spirit. It is only in Him and through Him that the miracle of new life takes place.

THE GIFT ABOVE ALL GIFTS

Today there is much talk of gifts, sometimes more than is good for our spiritual lives.

When we fix our gaze too firmly on the gifts, it is easy to lose sight of the giver.

Let us therefore take as the point of departure for our study the very heart of the gospel, John 3:16: "For God so loved the world, that he gave his only begotten Son, that whosoever believeth in him should not perish, but have everlasting life."

God gave the greatest gift that He had to give us, His only Son.

In this one gift is comprehended all that can serve for our eternal salvation.

Paul writes:
"He that spared not his own Son, but delivered him up for us all, how shall he not with him also freely give us all things?" (Rom. 8:32);
"But of him are ye in Christ Jesus, who of God is made unto us wisdom, and righteousness, and sanctification, and redemption" (I Cor. 1:30).

Everything—in *Him*, through *Him*, with *Him*.
Whoever accepts Jesus in faith will have opened to him a life of indescribable peace; to him heaven is opened while he is yet on this earth.

At this point I wish to recount one of my most recent experiences and tell how one person accepted the gift above all gifts, Jesus.

I must first give the background to this account. As a result of television and the terrible pressure of daily life in the modern world, almost no one reads books that discuss abstract biblical topics. Readers are also tired of looking up biblical citations in their Bibles. This is why the short Bible passages are cited in full in this book. In addition, many short accounts of personal experiences are brought in to avoid tiring the reader.

This book is being written in the house of my friend Gottfried Amend in Montreal, and in Nova Scotia.

During this lecture tour in the Canadian province of Quebec, I also had a long talk with Ives Petelle, who owns and operates a pizzeria in the provincial capital, Quebec. We had met once before, two years previously. In 1972 I held a conference with a French congregation. During the discussion, Ives Petelle, one of the participants, contradicted what I was saying. His major argument was: "I am a Christian and an astrologer." At that time I responded to the young long-haired man: "Please read Isaiah 47:13-14. There we find, among other things, 'Let now the astrologers, the star-gazers, the monthly prognosticators, stand up, and save thee from these things that shall come upon thee. Behold, they shall be as stubble; the fire shall burn them; they shall not deliver themselves from the power of the flame.' "

When I made this reply I could not suspect what effect these words might have. A year later, my friend Amend sent me the printed witness of this astrologer. The frontispiece is a photograph of him with long hair; on the back is a picture of him neatly dressed and with his hair cut. His testimony is titled *Pourquoi j'ai quitté l'Astrologie* ("Why I Turned My Back on Astrology"). In the course of his book, this disciple of Jesus terms that conference in Quebec the turning-point of his life.

That was in 1972, the period of my life when the waves of temptation were rolling over me and many of the faithful were "hitting me when I was down." In the midst of the worst agony the Lord can provide wonderful comfort.

But now the sequel to the Petelle story. At Bethel, a Bible college near Sherbrook, I had delivered several lectures. One of the students told me and my friend that he had found Jesus through Petelle. Twenty-two other young people like him had been set upon the way of life through the testimony of Petelle. Dr. Bard, the director of the school, therefore also invited Petelle to address the school.

That is not all. Petelle, the owner of a pizzeria, prays together with a room full of customers. And they put up with it. This young man shows unusual courage in confessing Jesus. Above all he warns his listeners against the very astrology he had formerly practiced, as well as against all kinds of occultism. It is as though God chose for me a young disciple.

Where the Spirit of God is at work and the seed of the gospel is sown and springs up, the Enemy does not look on idly. Consequently, Petelle became the subject of a counterattack. Satan knows how to treat believers. He does not use men of this world, but religious individuals.

This religious enemy came from Europe. Brother B. was visiting his son in Quebec and heard about Petelle. He warned this young witness to Jesus against me, advising him not to say anything ill about astrology and occultism, since that would without fail unleash violent attacks. It is true that to be attacked in the exercise of this ministry is only too common an occurrence. But what matters is not whether our vocation is hard or easy, but what the Lord wills. Today there are hundreds of thousands languishing in the chains of occultism, and there are very few pastors working in this area. What Brother B. had to say and his warnings produced an inner conflict in Petelle. I spoke with him about it as a pastor. In the kingdom of God it is a frequent experience for God to call a young witness and older believers to feel called upon to "quench the fire."

Jesus once said to His disciples: "But I say unto

you, That every idle word that men shall speak, they shall give account thereof in the day of judgment." (Matt. 12:36). Whoever experiences such things in the community of Jesus knows the value of Jesus to him.

Paul strengthens this wonderful assurance: "In [Jesus] we have redemption through his blood, the forgiveness of sins, according to the riches of his grace" (Eph. 1:7).

At the time of my greatest temptations, one of the brethren wrote to me: "Do not keep your gaze fixed on the believers, do not be caught up in your own mistakes and failings, but keep your gaze fixed on Jesus."

This brother is right. "How shall God not freely give us all things with his Son?" writes Paul.

In this promise everything is contained. In *Him* peace for the heart; in *Him* strength for the soul; in *Him* joy among tears; in *Him* security; in *Him* protection against all foes; in *Him* forgiveness, redemption, eternal salvation. Is Jesus not God's greatest gift?

THE REPRESENTATIVE OF JESUS

Whoever would learn about the representative of Jesus should read at his leisure and with prayer chapters 14—16 of the Gospel of John.

In these farewell discourses, Jesus promised His disciples in John 14:18: "I will not leave you comfortless."

Ten days after his ascension from this earth, the exalted Lord sent the Holy Spirit, the Pareclete, His representative.

What is the outstanding task of this representative?

In Acts 1:8, the Lord promised: "But ye shall receive power, after that the Holy Spirit is come upon you: and ye shall be witnesses unto *me*"

In John 14:26, we read: "But the Comforter, which is the Holy Spirit, whom the Father will send in *my* name, he shall teach you all things."

John 15:26 states: "but when the Comforter is come, whom I will send unto you from the Father,. . . he shall testify of me."

John 16:13-14 further confirms this points: "Howbeit when he, the Spirit of truth, is come, he will guide you into all truth. . . . He shall glorify *me:* for he shall receive of *mine*" (vv. 13, 14).

The first and greatest function of the Holy Spirit is the glorification of Jesus. He glorifies Jesus, He places Jesus in the midst of all that takes place.

When there is so much talk of gifts and Jesus recedes into the background, the Holy Spirit is not at work.

The ministry of the representative

Glorification of Jesus is the first point on the Holy Spirit's program. Then it is our turn.

The first thing He does to comfort us is to remain

with us. Jesus made this promise and fulfilled what He said in John 14:16: "I will pray the Father, and he shall give you another Comforter, that he may abide with you for ever."

Only those who are broken, tempted, trampled down know what the comfort of the Holy Spirit means.

In Psalm 119:92, the psalmist says: "Unless thy law had been my delights, I should then have perished in mine affliction."

King Hezekiah also knew this comfort. In Isaiah 38:17, he confessed: "Behold, for peace I had great bitterness: but thou hast in love to my soul delivered it from the pit of corruption: for thou hast cast all my sins behind thy back."

Part of this comfort is to represent us before the throne of God with unutterable groanings (Rom. 8:26), constantly to bring the Word of God to life for us (John 6:63), and give us the help we need. This last-named function must be described in the words of the Bible. We read in Philippians 1:18-19: "Every way . . . Christ is preached. . . . For I know that this shall turn to my salvation through your prayer, and the supply of the Spirit of Jesus Christ."

Here, too, we note the connection, observing that the activity of the Holy Spirit in the faithful is intimately linked with Jesus.

What is central must remain central, and must not be displaced by what is peripheral.

Our contact with the Holy Spirit

There is no way from us to the Holy Spirit, only a way from Him to us. Jesus said in John 3:8: "The wind bloweth where it listeth."

The Lord, however, has given us a possibility: we may pray for it. In Luke 11:13, we read: "How much more shall your heavenly Father give the Holy Spirit to them that ask him?" As mentioned already, such praying does not mean, however, that we may force something special from the Holy Spirit.

We do not need to ask for a new outpouring of the Holy Spirit. The Holy Spirit has been present since His outpouring on the first Day of Pentecost. He dwells in His community, in the hearts of His faithful people. We can only ask that the Holy Spirit will come to us and take possession of us.

His operation in us

This New Testament uses various expressions to describe the operation of the Holy Spirit in us. Eight of these will be mentioned.

1. "Except a man be *born again*, he cannot see the kingdom of God" (John 3:3). Rebirth, which is only accomplished by the grace of God, also gives us the Holy Spirit. "No man can say that Jesus is the Lord, but by the Holy Spirit" (I Cor. 12:3).
2. "He shall *baptize* you with the Holy Spirit, and with fire" (Matt. 3:11). The noun "baptism" of the Holy Spirit does not occur in the Bible. Six times, however, we find the verb "to baptize" with the Holy Spirit.
3. "On the Gentiles also was *poured out* the gift of the Holy Spirit" (Acts 10:45).
4. "Repent, and be baptized every one of you in the name of Jesus Christ for the remission of sins, and ye shall *receive* the gift of the Holy Spirit" (Acts 2:38).

5. " . . . that thou mightest receive thy sight, and be *filled* with the Holy Spirit" (Acts 9:17).
6. "If any man be in Christ, he is a *new creature*" (II Cor. 5:17). Here we find the work of renewal once again in connection with Christ, who gives the Holy Spirit.
7. "The Spirit itself *beareth witness* with our spirit, that we are the children of God" (Rom. 8:16).
8. Sealing through the Holy Spirit. On God's side the work of rebirth is complete and sufficient. Just as a newborn child is already perfectly developed and needs only to grow, so is rebirth a completed work of God. This fact is expressed by the term "sealing." "In whom also after that ye believed, ye were *sealed* with the holy Spirit of promise" (Eph. 1:13). "And grieve not the holy Spirit of God, whereby ye are *sealed* unto the day of redemption" (Eph. 4:30).

The doctrine of stages

The American pentecostal churches have developed a doctrine of stages out of the work of the Holy Spirit. It looks roughly this way: conversion —rebirth—baptism in the Spirit—gift of tongues —sinlessness, and so on.

In this unbiblical theology they support their position in part on historical developments in the time of Jesus. Let us take the life of the apostle Peter. Luke 5 reports how Peter came to confess his sinfulness. He followed after Jesus, but nevertheless denied Him in the courtyard while He was being tried, and finally ran away in terror from the foot of the cross. Not until Pentecost did he become a fearless witness and preach in foreign languages.

The experience of Peter in the course of his life is now reproduced as a doctrine of stages. This theology is naive and childish. In Luke 5, Jesus could not reveal the total plan of salvation to Peter because His death on the cross, His resurrection, His ascension, and Pentecost still lay in the future. Pentecost was in the future of Peter. We have it behind us.

I have read many American books about glossolalia. It is hard to get over one's astonishment at the audacity with which they pervert the Word of God and the history of the church.

In one book, for instance, we read: "Paul experienced his conversion on the road to Damascus, but only received his baptism in the Spirit through the laying on of hands of Brother Ananias."

In church history the pentecostals ascribe the gift of tongues to many great men of God in order to bolster their thesis. Even Luther, according to them, was among those who spoke in tongues. For example, on page 28 of Howard N. Ervin's *And Forbid not to Speak with Tongues* we read: "Martin Luther was a prophet, evangelist, speaker in tongues and interpreter in one person, endowed with all the gifts of the Spirit."

There is not room here to enter into a detailed discussion. Only one remark: they falsify the historical facts. Martin Luther and many other men of God did not speak in tongues.

Can the gift of the Spirit be repeated?

Can rebirth be repeated? No—no more than a child can return to his mother's womb and be born a second time.

Can rebirth be lost? Here American theologians

differ from their German counterparts. I rely on the saying in John 6:39: "And this is the Father's will which hath sent me, that of all which he hath given me I should lose nothing, but should raise it up again at the last day."

Can reborn Christians sin and play truant from the school of God? Yes.

Can they return to Jesus? Here, too, opinion in America differs from that in Germany. The Americans base their position on Hebrews 6:4-6 and 10:26-27. Discussion of these passages would go beyond the limits of this paperback.

In my pastoral work I would rather be guided by mercy than by hard sayings that express judgment. We read: "I will heal their backsliding" (Hos. 14:4); "Return, ye backsliding children, and I will heal your backslidings" (Jer. 3:22).

Can a Christian be guilty of the sin against the Holy Spirit?

Those Christians who come for pastoral counseling in fear and trembling, and confess: "I have committed the sin against the Holy Spirit," have beyond doubt not committed it; else they would not worry about it. The man who has really committed the sin against the Holy Spirit is spiritually dead and is no longer concerned about it.

But this question raises several problems. I do not know any reborn Christians who have committed the sin against the Holy Spirit, although I know backsliders in plenty.

In order to answer this question of the sin against the Holy Spirit, we must discuss Matthew 12:22-30. Jesus healed a man by driving out his demons. The Pharisees saw this and blasphemed: "This fellow doth not cast out devils, but by Beelzebub the prince of the devils" (v. 24). Here the Pharisees reached their conclusion in the face of better knowledge. They were undoubtedly familiar with Jewish exorcism. They had never assumed that a Jewish exorcist would undertake exorcisms in the name of the devil. In the case of Jesus, however, they refused to recognize this, because it would have meant recognizing His messianic status. Therefore they not only blasphemed against Jesus, but also against the Holy Spirit, through whose power He undertook the exorcisms.

The situation we face today is not the same. Jesus no longer stands visible in our midst. It is therefore no longer possible to blaspheme against Him personally and against His Holy Spirit.

For us, however, there are other opportunities for blasphemy. I will illustrate this by means of an example from my pastoral work. A woman about forty-five years old came to me for counseling. She confessed that when she was twenty she had felt strongly moved by the Holy Spirit. In the course of an evangelistic program she felt her conscience stricken. She realized that she would have to be converted. But she was in love with worldly pleasures. Above all, she liked to go dancing.

After one evening meeting, she came home, fell on her knees, and prayed after the following manner: "Lord, I know that I must come to you. But let me enjoy my youth. Later will be fine, when I am a few years older."

She resisted the movements of the Holy Spirit. A few years later she married. It was before the war. She came to an agreement with her husband that they would save up for a house before having children.

The man was drafted in the war and did not return. She lost the house because of the chances of war. In the midst of these disasters she began to search for God, but she had no success. During pastoral counseling, she broke down and wept, and confessed: "When I was twenty I refused to be converted. At first we wanted no children. Now I have lost my husband, my house, and even the possibility of having children. When I pray, it is as though there were a great gulf between God and me. I cannot get anywhere with my prayers."

Of course I tried to show this woman the way to Jesus. It was to no avail. I could not help her. It was uncanny. I asked myself whether this had been a sin against the Holy Spirit.

To resist the movements of the Holy Spirit deliberately year after year is dangerous. Grace has its limits and its proper hour. We must recognize the chance when it is given us. We cannot play games with the Lord, with His grace, and with the urgings of the Holy Spirit.

Strength in the Spirit

In Galatians 5:17, Paul states: "The flesh lusteth against the Spirit." In daily life our strength is worn down; we are continually defiled. Therefore we are admonished by the apostle: "If we live in the Spirit, let us also walk in the spirit" (Gal. 5:25). It is possible to quench the Spirit (I Thess. 5:19), to grieve the Spirit (Eph. 4:30).

When this happens, life in the Holy Spirit falters.

The healthy development is increasing strength in the Spirit. Paul writes: "For this cause I bow my knees unto the Father of our Lord Jesus Christ . . . that he would grant you, according to the riches of his glory, to be strengthened with might by his Spirit in the inner man" (Eph. 3:14, 16). This inner growth corresponds to the admonition in Ephesians 5:18: "Be filled with the Spirit."

Is this not at odds with the initial filling with the Holy Spirit? No, the New Testament contains several accounts of how disciples were repeatedly filled with the Holy Spirit. "[Jesus] breathed on them, and saith unto them, Receive ye the Holy Spirit" (John 20:22).

This was a kind of "down payment" against what was to come on Pentecost. "They were all filled with the Holy Spirit" (Acts 2:4); "When they had prayed, the place was shaken where they were assembled together; and they were all filled with the Holy Spirit" (Acts 4:31).

The great role played by the Holy Spirit in strengthening the inner man can be seen from the following biblical passages.

"And when they saw [Jesus], they worshipped him: but some doubted" (Matt. 28:17).

"And [the disciples], when they had heard that he was alive, and had been seen of [Mary Magdalene], believed not" (Mark 16:11).

"After that he appeared in another form unto two of [the Emmaus disciples], as they walked, and went into the country. And they went and told it unto the residue: neither believed they them" (Mark 16:12-13).

"Then [Jesus] said unto [the Emmaus disciples] O fools, and slow of heart to believe all that the prophets have spoken" (Luke 24:25).

"And while they yet believed not for joy, and wondered, [Jesus] said unto them, Have ye here any meat?" (Luke 24:41).

This was the attitude of the disciples who had not yet been given power and authority by the Holy Spirit. After Pentecost the situation was quite different.

"Then Peter, filled with the Holy Spirit, said unto them. . . ." (Acts 4:8).

"But [Stephen], being full of the Holy Spirit, looked up stedfastly into heaven" (Acts 7:55).

"For [Barnabas] was a good man, and full of the Holy Spirit and of faith" (Acts 11:24).

"Then Saul, (who also is called Paul,) filled with the Holy Spirit, set his eyes on him" (Acts 13:9).

"And the disciples were filled with joy, and with the Holy Spirit" (Acts 13:52).

The Holy Spirit changes the whole situation. He changes men's characters, changes their motives. He inspires, He leads into all truth, He determines God's will. He enables weak instruments to perform great deeds. He makes up for our insufficiency with His power and authority. It is He who strengthens us spiritually for service.

THE EVOLUTION OF THE GIFTS OF GRACE

The title of this book speaks of "gifts of the Spirit." The title of this chapter uses the expression "gifts of grace." In order to avoid confusion, the Greek original will be cited.

Terminology

In I Corinthians 12:1, the apostle uses the term *pneumatika*, which means spiritual gifts. The source of these gifts is the *pneuma*, the Holy Spirit. Since the Holy Spirit is given to men at their rebirth—and of course also at later times when they receive a greater infilling of the Spirit—only someone who is reborn can receive the gifts of the Holy Spirit and have them develop within him.

In I Corinthians 12:4, Paul speaks of *charismata*, the gifts of grace. *Charis* means grace. This expression therefore means that the grace of God bestows these spiritual gifts. It is therefore proper to speak of both the gifts of the Spirit and the gifts of grace.

The different sources of the gifts

Since the Christian congregations today are afflicted with a thousandfold confusion, it is frequently appropriate to speak of the source of spiritual gifts.

Roughly speaking, the problem of gifts is threefold. First, there are gifts and abilities that come from above. They are bestowed on the believer by the Holy Trinity. These gifts frequently lie hidden in someone who has been reborn; they must be brought to light and developed.

In this context, Paul admonishes his friend and fellow worker Timothy: "I put thee in remembrance that thou stir up the gift of God, which is in thee by the putting on of my hands" (II Tim. 1:6). He also writes: "Neglect not the gift that is in thee, which was given thee by prophecy, with the laying on of hands of the presbytery" (I Tim. 4:14).

Second, man cannot have gifts of the Holy Spirit, but he can have natural talent, natural gifts determined by heredity. Great men such as Aristotle, Goethe, and Einstein have had natural endowments that are almost superhuman. But these supermen did not have the gifts of the Holy Spirit.

When men so richly endowed accept the living God in faith, they receive in addition gifts from above. Their natural talents can also be purified by the Spirit of God and utilized by Him.

An example from the world of music may illustrate this principle. Musical talent can be used for the glory of God or in the service of sin. In Rio de Janeiro or Bahia in Brazil, for example, the Macumba spiritualists use rock and roll music to produce a state of ecstasy that often ends in a sexual orgy.

But musical talent can also be used in the service of God. I cite the *Passions* by Johann Sebastian Bach, or the *Messiah* by Handel. Handel wrote the *Messiah* in twenty-three days, an incredible feat that could be accomplished only with inspiration from above.

While he was composing it, Handel scarcely took time to eat or sleep. When he had completed the oratorio, he was found weeping in his workroom. It is a work of music that moves the listener to worship.

Besides the gifts and endowments that are divine and those that are human, there is a third category: demonic gifts, which in our own day have increasingly confused mankind. The demonic gifts, which have Satan as their source, include all magical and spiritualistic powers. Satan acts as God's antagonist; for each of the gifts of the Spirit and for each miracle in the Bible he introduces a demonic counterpart. These satanic miracles are often served up to men in the guise of true spiritual nourishment, so that many are led astray. We must take note of II Corinthians 11:13-15: "For such are false apostles, deceitful workers, transforming themselves into the apostles of Christ. And no marvel; for Satan himself is transformed into an angel of light. Therefore it is no great thing if his ministers also be transformed as the ministers of righteousness."

Without my wishing it so, it has become part of my vocation in life to lay bare these outwardly religious satanic gifts and warn against them. This task, which I did not seek out, has almost cost me my life. I have had to face inconceivable attacks and ambushes from the Archenemy. I wish I had never heard of these satanic gifts.

The question is whether these satanic gifts, like the gifts and talents that are naturally inherited, can be purified and used for God's purposes. There are inexperienced theologians and preachers who would answer yes. My experience during forty-five

83

years of pastoral work shows that it is totally impossible. One can only be set free from the powers of Satan through Christ, never purify them and use them for God's kingdom. On this point I must issue the most radical warning conceivable.

For orientation in this matter and a more detailed discussion, the reader should consult my book *Demonism, Past and Present*. This book contains a chapter on the difference between spiritual gifts, natural gifts, and demonic gifts.

In this present chapter, then, we will maintain the threefold distinction: there are gifts from above, gifts from below, and human gifts.

Mediumistic gifts

The most difficult task is to determine the nature of mediumistic gifts. The very term raises difficulties. It comes from the Latin word *medium*, which means middle.

This term is also used for intermediaries in spiritism. A medium establishes the link between us and unknown forces, realms, or spirits. The energy released is called "mediumistic." The term "ESP" is along the same line.

The status of a medium can be acquired in three ways. It can be inherited, it can be acquired through magical or spiritistic experiments, and it can be gained through transference.

Occult experimentation and transference are both an offense and a burden, although they frequently come about through ignorance.

One inherits mediumistic gifts as an aftereffect of sins committed by one's ancestors in practicing sorcery. This form of endowment is often unknown to those who have it. Initially, there is no offense involved, since, for example, a great-grandson cannot be held responsible for the actions of his great-grandfather. Mediumistic abilities are inherited through the fourth generation, and thus fulfill the first commandment. Even if they do not represent a direct offense, they are nevertheless a burden. Anyone who puts this inherited gift once more into practice commits an offense.

We must therefore maintain the following position: the inherited mediumistic ability is not an offense, only a burden. It is not in itself demonic, but opens the door to demonic influences. But it becomes a demonic burden when it is put into practice. For this reason the Christian who discovers that he has inherited such an ability must ask God to take it from him and bestow on him instead the power of the Holy Spirit.

The Holy Spirit has nothing to do with the realm of mediumistic power. His realm is the pneumatic realm, the realm of inspiration and charisma. This is the realm we will now address.

THE VARIETY OF MINISTRIES

All the gifts that the Holy Spirit bestows serve to build up the community of Jesus. In I Corinthians 12:7, Paul writes: "But the manifestation of the Spirit is given to every man to profit withal."

Peter furnishes the same admonition in I Peter 4:10: "As every man hath received the gift, even so minister the same one to another."

Anyone whose spiritual gifts lead him into religious pride has already lost them.

On the Ivory Coast I was delivering lectures at various mission stations. In the vicinity of Zouenula, one missionary complained to me: "We have here a missionary who asserts that he has all nine gifts of the Spirit mentioned in I Corinthians 12:7-11. At the same time, he is the most difficult of the brethren here. He is dogmatic, inflexible, intolerant, contentious. That is not how the gifts of the Spirit operate."

In the following discussion of the individual gifts, we will simply follow the various texts that speak of these gifts. In the individual texts we will not discuss those gifts that have been discussed in the preceding text. The texts in question are these: I Corinthians 12:7-11; I Corinthians 12:28-31; Romans 12:6-10; Ephesians 4:11; I Peter 4:10-11.

1. The fulness (pleroma) of gifts in Jesus

We have already spoken of Jesus as the gift above all gifts. In Him is opened to us the entire wealth of the Father and the Holy Spirit. We must call this fact to mind once more:

"I am come that they might have life, and that they might have it *more abundantly*" (John 10:10).

"For in [Jesus] dwelleth all the *fulness* of the Godhead bodily" (Col. 2:9).

"My people shall be *satisfied* with my goodness" (Jer. 31:14). [In the Hebrew text: gifts of fulness.]

"And of his *fulness* have all we received, and grace for grace" (John 1:16).

All our discussion of spiritual gifts must take place under the guidance of the Holy Spirit and with our gaze fixed on Jesus; otherwise we will go astray from the sound biblical course.

2. Wisdom (sophia)

As a spiritual gift, wisdom does not mean a man's natural intellectual abilities, however brilliant he may be. Paul had harsh words to say about the wisdom of this world, because this human wisdom has often boasted itself superior to the wisdom of God. He states: "I will destroy the wisdom of the wise, and will bring to nothing the understanding of the prudent. . . . Where is the disputer of this world? hath not God made foolish the wisdom of this world? For after that in the wisdom of God the world by wisdom knew not God, it pleased God by the foolishness of preaching to save them that believe" (I Cor. 1:19-21). And, "Professing themselves to be wise, they became fools" (Rom. 1:22).

Theological education, whether in universities or seminaries, has often followed this false trail of human wisdom. Theological teachers without the Holy Spirit render their students spiritually sterile, which means they bear no spiritual fruit.

I have often used the following image: "A garbageman with the Holy Spirit gets more out of the Bible than a theologian without the Holy Spirit."

Of course we are doubly grateful when a

theologian also has the Holy Spirit. One such man was my own teacher, mentioned above, Prof. Karl Heim of Tübingen, who as a young man found the way to Jesus through the famous evangelist Elias Schrenk.

The wisdom and inspiration bestowed by the Holy Spirit is different in character. Three of its features will be illustrated by these texts:

1. "But we speak the wisdom of God in a mystery, even the hidden wisdom, which God ordained before the world unto our glory" (I Cor. 2:7).
2. "But the wisdom that is from above is first pure, then peaceable, gentle, and easy to be intreated, full of mercy and good fruits" (James 3:17).
3. "He that winneth souls is wise" (Prov. 11:30).

The wisdom from above gives us access to the hidden counsels of God, makes us shine forth, and is active in the salvation of souls.

3. Knowledge (gnosis)

The Greek word for knowledge, *gnosis*, does not have a good reputation in the history of theology. Two centuries were filled with so-called gnostic speculations. This gnosis still haunts our century as the doctrine of eons in the heads of the Universal Reconcilers. In every age human knowledge has refused to remain obedient to God, degenerating instead into false doctrine and heresy.

We may say roughly the same thing about knowledge as we do about wisdom. Not even a universal genius, not even the human "brains" of all the nations, can know God.

Without the Holy Spirit we wander in darkness, even when we succeed in building interstellar spaceships and traveling beyond the limits of our solar system.

Only the knowledge given by the Holy Spirit can plumb the regions of God beyond the limits of the cosmos. Paul describes this in the Epistle to the Colossians: "to the acknowledgement of the mystery of God, and of the Father, and of Christ; In whom are hid all the treasures of wisdom and knowledge" (2:2-3).

This knowledge of God also has a practical side for the faithful. Let me give two examples.

The famous inventor known as "Steamer Smith" was a faithful Christian. He had no higher education, but was still able to register 120 patents. He was once asked how he could be responsible for so many discoveries and inventions without being a professional engineer. He replied: "I took the problems to bed with me, prayed about them at length, reflected on them, and the next morning the secret was revealed to me." Here we have an example of the Holy Spirit using human ability and adding His own knowledge.

Another example is much closer to me. I would like to speak of a man for whose friendship over many years I will once more express my gratitude, Dr. M. Out of modesty he wishes to remain anonymous. He worked for years as a specialist in quartz glass; he did not have an equal anywhere in the world. Years ago he developed the formula for a prism of quartz glass that makes it possible to reflect a beam of light that strikes the prism back to its source even when the prism changes its angle of incidence as much as fifteen degrees. Hardly a single reader will realize what I am saying here in the words of a layman. But the Russians and Americans quickly realized how important it was. The Russians offered Dr. M. six million dollars for this formula. He refused to sell it. The Americans made Dr. M. director of a quartz glass company in New Jersey—even though he is a German—in order to get the formula. Here, too, the inventor had reservations. In one case, the reflectors of Dr. M. rest today on the moon. The Americans bought these quartz prisms, developed by Dr. M. They have since been performing their function at the lunar station built by the Americans.

Now comes the important point. I asked Dr. M., "How did you discover this formula?" He replied, "Through prayer."

We have spoken of two inventors who were undoubtedly gifted with technical genius. But the Holy Spirit added to their talent the gift of "knowledge from above," which was given in prayer.

4. Faith (pistis)

Every Christian who follows Jesus practices faith. Without faith there is no forgiveness of sins. Without faith there is no assurance of eternal life. "Without faith it is impossible to please [God]" (Heb. 11:6).

When faith is mentioned in the list of gifts of the Spirit, this does not mean the justifying faith that everyone must have who yearns for eternal life. The faith that comes as a gift of the Spirit is the daring and conquering faith that removes mountains. Many great works of the kingdom of God have been accomplished by men with daring faith. I may recall the orphanages of George Müller in Bristol. Or remember the life and work of Hudson Taylor, who showed millions of Chinese the way to Jesus. Think also of Dwight Moody, whose work brings blessings to thousands, even today. I am also pleased to recall the founders and fathers of the Chrishona Mission in Switzerland, and of the Liebenzell and Marburg Missions in Germany.

It is not only great accomplishments that have their history of faith; minor events can also lie on the same plane. There are men with five pounds, but there are also those with fewer pounds and a smaller radius. One such minor venture in faith should be mentioned.

It was several years back. Wolfgang Heiner, the founder and leader of the "Good News" missionary group, reached an agreement with me to start a large-scale evangelization program in Karlsruhe, the largest city in my area. We planned to rent the most spacious hall in the city, the Black Forest Auditorium. The next step was to gain the support of the local clergy for this undertaking. We therefore asked that this evangelistic enterprise be announced from the pulpit, in addition to public advertising.

Then came the first harassment in the form of Bishop Bender, who was then bishop of the region. At a clergy conference in my very presence he spoke out against this proposed program of evangelism.

In spite of this cold shower we continued with our plans. Then came the second obstacle. In a private session of all the participants, the chief of the city pastors, Dr. Kohnlein, asked who would be responsible for the resulting deficit. Dr. Kohnlein understood our project. As chief administrator, he had to protect the local church from any repercussions. In response to his question about finances, I stated bluntly, "If it is God's will for us to carry out this fishing expedition on a great scale, He will supply us with what is needed. I will add, however, that I am ready personally to be responsible for the deficit, even if I should have to sell my house to meet it." To my friend Wolfgang Heiner I confided later, "I will keep my house. We don't have a stingy God."

The evangelistic campaign went well. In the evening there were four thousand in the hall. We therefore planned to extend the campaign through Holy Week.

When we announced this intention we were vetoed by Bishop Bender, who stated: "Holy Week should be observed with silence, not with uproar." This was puzzling, for we had given him no ground for making such a statement.

We did not give up our plan to extend our mission at once, but fought for this third week. Above all I recall with gratitude young Pastor Katz, who was not afraid of the bishop and supported us vigorously. He stated: "Karlsruhe has thirty-eight pulpits; why shouldn't there be a thirty-ninth pulpit in the Black Forest Auditorium during Holy Week? We must be grateful for every opportunity to preach the Word." Our wish was not granted. We had to interrupt our sacred work. Our hearts were left bleeding.

Something must now be said about the financial

arrangements, because the church had grave reservations on this point. We had called upon famous evangelists. Among them were Major Ian Thomas, the founder of the Torchbearers; Anton Schulte, the founder of the missionary society New Life; and Dr. Bergmann, the champion of the German evangelists. They received transportation plus an honorarium that was not stingy, but generous. Now we waited with bated breath. Would expenses be met or not? Could we pay for the hall—whose rent was considerable, for all the newspaper ads, for the hundred thousand fliers, for the hundreds of posters, along with the rental of billboard space?

The tally showed expenses of nearly sixteen thousand dollars. In the circumstances of Germany in 1956 that was an enormous sum. It is no empty statement but the simple truth: Wolfgang Heiner and I were not worried for a moment about the financial outcome. Both of us know something firsthand about the faithfulness of God and the certainty of His promises. The offerings totaled eighteen thousand dollars, giving a surplus of two thousand dollars. The "Good News" missionary group used it to buy a loudspeaker for its automobile.

The faith that ventured everything on Jesus had triumphed. This account is not meant to glorify our faith. It is true enough that on other occasions we lost heart and gave up in despair. No, here we see only the question addressed by Jesus to His disciples: "Lacked ye any thing?" (Luke 22:35). The disciples replied: "Nothing." Are we not willing to undertake the venture of faith with this Jesus?

In this context it is good to read prayerfully Hebrews 11, the chapter about faith. It will give us an incentive to cast all our cares, small and great, on Him who never fails His children.

These stories are being written down in the house of Mr. and Mrs. Fred Thomas, in Woodstock, Canada. During the past two days this family has become a special experience of faith for us. Once again, this fact will be set down in print to glorify the fidelity of God. I had traveled from Germany to Canada in order to speak before a Bible college, among other engagements. My friend and organizer Gottfried Amend accompanied me on a long and tiring trip by car from Montreal to New Brunswick and Nova Scotia. We had put more than 1,800 miles behind us.

When we arrived, we were so exhausted that I had to lie down right away. In the meanwhile, my friend had spoken with the director of the Bible college, and brought back word, which he reported with distress, that I would not be permitted to speak. What had happened? A German-Canadian living in Germany had "prepared" the director. This misguided Christian thought he was doing God and the Bible college a favor. This door had been slammed shut.

A family of believers heard of my visit, came more than sixty miles to get me, and took me back with them to speak in their church. They quickly prepared hand-lettered signs and displayed them in the stores. In addition, they organized a direct transmission over the radio. Within twenty-four hours they got up an effective advertising campaign, and the Lord blessed all their efforts.

This served greatly to strengthen my faith as well

as that of my organizer. We were certain that we could never have done as well on our own as the Lord had done.

When the devil shuts a door, the Lord can open a great gate. It would do us no harm to have this repeated.

We have a God who performs miracles. His service leads to glorious experiences.

> If thou but suffer God to guide thee,
> And hope in Him through all thy ways,
> He'll give thee strength whate'er betide thee,
> And bear thee through the evil days.
> Who trusts in God's unchanging love
> Builds on a rock that nought can move.

5. Healing gifts (charismata iamaton)

The subject of faith healing today is a source of great uncertainty and confusion for the faithful.

First a word against legalistic restrictions. Naturally believing Christians can call on physicians for help. God gave us our reason in order for us to use it. Faith healing and medical help are not contradictory, as extremists frequently assert.

With respect to practitioners of faith healing, caution is indicated. There are those who practice occultism, though of course there are also men who stay within the limits of this natural world and do not take advantage of any mediumistic abilities to transcend these limits. Unfortunately there are also doctors who occasionally recommend magical methods of healing in addition. In Schleswig, Germany, for example, I heard several times that doctors would sometimes send patients with shingles to magical practitioners. Schulz, the Provost of Hamburg, reported to me years ago that a member of his congregation had been referred by a doctor to such a sorcerer.

The question of faith healing has been outflanked by two extreme views.

The strict dispensationalists in the United States and Canada are of the opinion that some gifts of the Spirit are only temporary and ceased at the end of the apostolic age.

The extremists of the other school maintain that the so-called gift of tongues occurs in the same fashion today as in the apostolic age. Many of these emotionalists even insist that the gift of tongues is a demonstration of baptism in the Spirit.

Here in the context of faith healing we must state our own position on this question.

There is more biblical truth on the side of dispensational theology. During the apostolic period the New Testament was not yet extant. Jesus performed many miracles as signs of His messianic office. The apostles had miraculous powers and gifts of the Holy Spirit as proof of their apostolic commission. These were given to them not only as divine credentials, but also because the suffering of the people around them touched their hearts.

From the moment that the New Testament canon—that is, the whole New Testament—was extant, miraculous powers began to take a back seat to the inspired Word of God.

This decrease in the gifts of the Spirit can already be observed in the apostolic age. The last mention we hear of the gift of tongues is in the Epistle to the

Corinthians. In the later epistles of Paul and John it is not mentioned.

The situation is similar with respect to the gift of healing. In Acts 19:11-12, we read: "And God wrought special miracles by the hands of Paul: So that from his body were brought unto the sick hand-kerchiefs or aprons, and the diseases departed from them, and the evil spirits went out of them."

Fourteen years later, however, Paul could no longer heal his fellow workers. We read: "For indeed he [Epaphroditus] was sick nigh unto death" (Phil. 2:27)' "Trophimus have I left at Miletum sick" (II Tim. 4:20).

This evolution was not only seen in the correct light by the dispensationalists. It was already being taught by the theological faculties of the European universities before there was a dispensational theology in the United States.

In North America I have frequently met proponents of this theology who state that these "temporary gifts of the Spirit" ceased totally in the apostolic age. This brings us into conflict with what happens in revivals and with the work of missionaries.

We must compose a response to both extreme flanks:

To the radical dispensationalists we must say: "Even if we do not possess the same miraculous gifts as the apostolic age, the Holy Spirit still did not shut up shop during the course of the first century. In individual instances, especially during revivals, the gifts of the Spirit break forth repeatedly. We have the same God and the same promises as the apostles, but not the same commission."

To the emotionalists we must say: "Stay sober and

rely on the fully inspired Word of God, not on your own emotional life. There are today thousands of biblically minded preachers of the gospel who nevertheless do not possess the gifts of healing and of tongues, but are more utilized by the Lord than spiritual agitators."

What must give pause to the two hostile camps is the experience of the great revivals. Here there takes place on a small scale what took place during the greatest of all revivals on the first Pentecost in Jerusalem.

Revivals among civilized peoples who have the Bible are usually not accompanied by great miracles. These people have the Word of God and have medical doctors for the sick. Of course their prayers are still heard, as are the prayers of all faithful Christians.

Revivals among primitive peoples, who do not have the Bible and cannot even read, are usually accompanied by great miracles of the Lord.

The best example is the revival on Timor (in Indonesia). At this point I must report something sad. Everywhere I go in the United States, Canada, or England, and even in Australia, the confidence believers might have in my book *The Revival in Indonesia* has been destroyed by an untruthful report on the part of an instructor at Dallas Theological Seminary. The sales of the book dropped at once, as my American publisher reported to me. The erroneous statements have been spread abroad by this report throughout the entire world.

A leader of the revival movement from Soe told me that this instructor spent only four days at Soe, the center of the revival. Furthermore, he did not go there until 1970, when the time of great miracles was already past. I myself was in Indonesia five times between 1963 and 1969, not only in Soe, but also in the areas of the revival that this instructor did not even visit, such as the island of Rote and West Irian. If I total up the length of time I spent in Indonesia, I was there twenty times as long as this critic. He wrote very boldly in his article "Indonesia Revival, True or False" (which is itself totally false): "Dr. Koch came much too late to Indonesia, never saw a miracle, and only listened to tapes." Through the goodness of God I shared the experience of great miracles. I did not listen to a single tape. I am curious to know why this man, who says he is a Christian, disseminates such obvious falsehoods about me. These sentences are being written in Nova Scotia, in the home of Pastor Ernest H. Nickerson, who told me, "In this country all confidence in your book on Indonesia has been lost."

The Timor revival is a perfect example of how God frames His plans. The people who live in the jungle do not have any schools. Only the large settlements like Kupang, Soe, Niki-Niki, and Atambua have schools. There are hundreds of thousands of Timorese who cannot read or write. To these illiterates God revealed Himself through miracles in the great revival, which began in 1965. But when the people who were illiterate learned to read and had received thousands of New Testaments and Bibles, miracles soon faded into the background.

Here, then, we face the same problem as in the apostolic age: miracles are the precursors until the written, printed, inspired Word of God is available. It is always a healthy development when the faithful learn to rely on the Word of God and not on their own experiences.

With reference to the gift of healing, it may be reported with gratitude that in connection with the Timor revival thousands of miraculous healings took place.

The teacher Ratu Alu on Timor had an extraordinary gift of healing. In 1964 he was able to help thousands. Unfortunately he became proud and lost his power, which was not restored to him despite his repentance.

In the course of the first evangelization campaign on Niki-Niki, undertaken by the first team, Superintendent Daniel reports that thousands were converted and some seven hundred of the sick were healed.

Specific gifts of healing, however, are very rare. In the nineteenth century, Pastor Blumhardt in Germany possessed such a gift.

At the present time there are many rumors of faith healers. In actual fact I am scarcely familiar with a single person at present who possesses a genuine gift of healing.

Of course there are many men of God who follow James 5:14 without any publicity and are given the experience of healing through faith. It is a real incentive for the life of faith to know that our God hears the entreaties of His children even in the twentieth century. For years the conclusion of Psalm 91 has been a great comfort to me.

Because he hath set his love upon me, therefore will I deliver him:
I will set him on high, because he hath known my name.

He shall call upon me, and I will answer him:
I will be with him in trouble;
I will deliver him, and honour him.
With long life will I satisfy him, and show him my
    salvation.

Like the other gifts of the Spirit, the gift of healing is exposed to great confusion. Matthew 24:24, in the Greek original, uses the expression *semeia kai terata,* "signs and wonders." This combination is found exclusively with reference to the activity of false Christs and false prophets. It is therefore a theological principle that signs and wonders are ambivalent. This means they can be from above or from below.

Today it must even be said that signs and wonders are trivalent. They can derive from three different sources, can have three different forces behind them. The threefold nature of this problem has already been discussed. It is best elucidated by three examples:

1. Among the Wallamo in southern Ethiopia, a Christian who had been blind for sixteen years received his sight through prayer and the laying on of hands of the elders (James 5:14).
   This was a biblical, divine healing. I have already discussed it in my book on Ethiopia.
2. Among primitive peoples there is also a form of blindness that is psychogenic, hysterical, and can be healed by suggestion. That is a healing of the blind on human terms.
3. Through confession I have heard of an instance when a blind girl was healed through black magic. This is a healing on demonic terms.

101

Once more we find the trichotomy: divine —human—demonic.

I have already discussed these questions in several paperbacks. The English titles are *Occult Bondage and Deliverance* and *Demonism, Past and Present*.

Space limitations prevent the mention of titles in other languages. Information about them can be obtained from Kregel Publications, Box 2607, Grand Rapids, Michigan 49501, and Hanssler-Verlag, 7303 Neuhausen a.F., Germany.

Since what has been stated in other publications cannot be repeated, an outline will be given here.

Healings on the divine plane

a. Through an explicit gift of healing (I Cor. 12:9).
b. Laying on of hands, anointing, and prayer by the elders of the community (James 5:14).
c. Simple prayer using the promises of God.

Healings on a more or less human plane

Suggestion—autosuggestion—religious suggestion—autogenic training—healing through meditation—hypnosis—healing through natural magnetism, and so forth.

Healings with demonic background

White magic—black magic—spiritistic and spiritualistic healing—fetishistic and psychometric healing—occult mental suggestion—hypnosis with an occult basis—occult magnetopathy.

How confused and unbiblical many healing

movements have become will be illustrated by means of a few examples.

Since my lecture ministry has taken me to every continent, I have a broad knowledge of unusual healings. Throughout the world blessed handkerchiefs are distributed to the sick in order to restore them to health. This practice is erroneously based on Acts 19:12. Since I have referred to it in other books, I will only make the following remark: handkerchiefs have the same qualities they had 1,900 years ago. All that is lacking is apostles with authority.

An original way of undertaking healings was reported to me in the United States by a Baptist minister. In the course of an assembly in Florida, the famous healer O. R. stated: "Today I want an original sacrifice. The ushers will now collect all the handkerchiefs, whether they are clean or not."

This was done. Then he prayed over the handkerchiefs and offered them back to heal the sick at a quarter a piece. Not everyone who wanted one was able to buy one, because there were not enough.

Other methods employed by the same healer are even more dubious. I have an issue of *Abundant Life* dated March 1971. In it there is a page of prayers with the picture of the publisher. The accompanying text contains the following instructions: "Use this page as your point of contact . . . to receive your miracle from God."

These healing tricks are very similar to psychometric healing.

The same issue contains the story of how a sick girl put a book by the same healer under her pillow in order to be healed. This procedure is very close to white magic.

What does all of this have to do with Jesus? Is it meant to have some sort of relationship to the charisma of healing? No, it has nothing to do with the Bible, but with witchcraft under pious disguise.

It is a necessary but unrewarding business to have to draw attention so often to unbiblical movements. Therefore our chapter on healing will conclude with a positive report.

One of my friends, Dr. Otto Riecker, published a book called *Summons from Indonesia.* Beginning on p. 75, Petrus Oktavianus recounts a healing. (This brother is called Pak Elias in my Indonesia book.) Oktavianus is presumably familiar to all Western critics as the best educated and most authoritative evangelist of Indonesia. Therefore this Indonesian brother will give Western observers an irrefutable demonstration. I quote:

"The Lord is also Lord of our bodies. He heals our diseases. He does so down to this very day. I myself do not have the commission and the gift from the Lord to emphasize healing in the preaching of the gospel. Only once in my entire ministry has a healing taken place, when I was challenged by Muslims. I prayed and had to say to the Lord, 'Lord, show the Muslims here that you are the Son of God, that you are a living and risen Lord, by means of a healing.' I had never before prayed in public for a sick man. Nevertheless, on the last day of the evangelistic campaign, I was bold enough to say, 'Bring the sick.' On the basis of my own previous experience I did not really have the courage to do so, because I do not have any gift for healing. But that day the Lord gave me visibly a powerful suggestion and also the freedom to do this.

"What happened? On that last day they brought the sick. The Lord guided me not to be His instrument for curing these people by myself. Instead, we all engaged in prayer so that the people wouldn't say that I was a great Christian magician. Therefore all of us who were present for this assembly prayed together. Then, in the name of the whole congregation and in the name of Jesus Christ, I commanded the disease to begone. That evening there were about thirty sick people whom the Lord healed of various diseases. The Lord has given me this gift only once in the course of my ministry, so that in this instance it might be demonstrated before the Muslims that Jesus is really the Son of God."

6. Miracles (energemata dynameon) (I Cor. 12:10)

Literally translated, this gift of the Holy Spirit means "works of power." Once again, we are not concerned with bodily strength; otherwise every winner in the Olympics would rank first. No, here we are concerned with expression of the power of the Holy Spirit.

There has been much theological debate about the nature of miracles. Let me mention only the scholastic argument between Thomas Aquinas and Anselm of Canterbury: are miracles within the natural realm or not?

Rationalists today, whether theologians or non-theologians, deny the existence of miracles. The orthodox admit the possibility of miracles in principle, but deny them when they are actually confronted with them in the present.

The biblical firebrands, on the contrary, have a mania for miracles. Between these two extremes of rationalistic denial and emotional exuberance a sound biblical course must be plotted.

Our faith does not live by miracles and the need for them, but by the Word of God. It does, however, live from the greatest miracle of all, the incarnation of the Son of God. It lives from what He did on the cross, from His resurrection, and from the gift of His Holy Spirit. It lives from the hope of His return and the saving will of God.

We must not be greedy for miracles, but must also not stand in God's way if He does something extraordinary.

Enough of theory. The place was West Irian, in the former capital Hollandia, now called Djajapura. Petrus Oktavianus was addressing some three to five thousand people at an outdoor assembly. Dark clouds were forming. A tropical storm was threatening, which within a few seconds would leave not a thread dry. This rain would have dispersed the assembly. Oktavianus saw in it an attack by the powers of darkness. In the name of Jesus he commanded the lowering clouds not to drop their burden on the assembly. And the Lord acknowledged his bold act of faith. During the same lecture series a violent storm set in. The corrugated iron houses built by the Dutch, with their loose roofs, presented a terrifying spectacle. The listeners could no longer understand the speaker. Once more Oktavianus gave command to the storm in the name of Jesus. And the storm abated.

The witnesses who will attest to this event are Petrus Oktavianus and Willi Haseloh, the missionary who was accompanying him. I have the story from them personally.

I have already reported this example in my book *Uns, Herr, wirst du Frieden schaffen* (p. 452).

Along with several other missionaries, I can personally attest to another experience during the Indonesia revival.

It was July 18, 1969—during my fifth visit to Indonesia. Together with an international team I was participating in the Lord's Supper in the church in Soe on Timor. During this service, the exalted Lord transformed water into wine. I was sitting with Petrus Oktavianus in the first pew. I have already reported this experience twice. Here I will only name the witnesses: Petrus Oktavianus, the leader of the JPPII Missionary Society; Prof. Daniel Baksch, a psychiatrist from Pakistan; Prof. Iqbal Nisar, head of a theological seminary in Pakistan; Prof. Shimizu, instructor at the University of Tokyo, Japan; and David Mitchell, an American missionary, along with others.

There were also many national witnesses, including some who are highly educated, like the governor, King Kusa Nope.

These witnesses are mentioned because Dr. Frank L. Cooley, one of the critics of my book on Indonesia, has written that he could not find any witnesses to the water-into-wine miracle. He need only have asked the local pastor, Pastor Daniel, or the governor's secretary Litteloni, who were part of the inner prayer circle when this miracle occurred on July 18, 1969.

I know for a fact that the leading brethren in Soe have learned to be afraid of all shades of critics. In a letter from Pastor Daniel I read the momentous statement that the visits of critics have become a serious problem for the revival movement.

God bestowed His miracles on the simple illiterate population in the jungle villages because they could not read the Bible. And now Western theologians, missionaries, and other visitors come and tear the wonderful acts of God to pieces through discussion, analysis, and criticism. Thus the devil has succeeded in his purpose of bringing this revival to a halt. The great period of miracles was already fading between 1968 and 1969, although as late as 1970 isolated instances of the Lord's power appeared.

7. Prophecies (propheteia)

No one need take offense at our enumeration of the gifts of the Spirit. It is unimportant whether we find nine or more in the various texts. My arriving at twenty-four is due to my exhaustive treatment of all the texts in question and the inclusion of Jesus as the first and greatest gift.

In order not to go astray from the very outset, we must make a fundamental distinction between "prophecy from above" and "soothsaying from below."

The subject of soothsaying cannot be discussed here. The reader may consult my books *Between Christ and Satan* or *Devil's Alphabet*.

The theme of prophecy is very extensive. Therefore only an outline will be given here.

Prophecy in the Old Testament

1. The prophets have a spiritual insight into the

circumstances of the day. Jeremiah, for example, told the king, the princes, and the people: "The Babylonians will take our city. It is better to surrender in advance to avoid unnecessary bloodshed."

2. Through inspiration, the prophets can see into the future. Consider, for example, the messianic prophecies (Servant Songs) in Isaiah 42, 49, 50, and 53.

3. Through inspiration, the prophets can make specific statements about a person's fate. Jeremiah, for example, was able to predict to the false prophet Hananiah that he would die during the current year; this in fact took place (Jeremiah 28).

4. To be a prophet could also mean to lay bare a concealed offense at the command of God. This is what Nathan did for David (II Samuel 12).

The prophetic gift in the New Testament

1. To speak as a prophet means to speak to the moment, like Peter in Acts 2, Stephen in Acts 7, and Paul in Acts 17.

2. To speak as a prophet means to reveal the future. The Revelation of John is the most powerful work predicting the future.

3. A prophet can also predict events in the near future. Agabus predicts the famine that occurred under the emperor Claudius (Acts 11:28). He also prophesies Paul's arrest in Jerusalem (Acts 21:10-11), which took place.

4. Prophetic insight also brings hidden offenses to light, as in the case of Peter with Ananias and Sapphira in Acts 5.

1. Prophetic revelation with respect to divine history, the return of Jesus, and the events of the eschaton ceased with the formation of the canon. Everything we have to know about the end is contained in the Bible, inspired by God. All this nonsense in extremist circles about "prophecies" concerning God's work in history is devoid of significance.

2. Occasionally a temporary prophetic gift, limited to a short period, can see some of the immediate future without being soothsaying. Here caution is indicated, because soothsayers usually present their satanically inspired power as the Spirit of God. A positive example deserves mention.

   There was a missionary conference in southern France. During the prayer assembly one of the brethren suddenly stood up and said to one of the other participants: "I saw you in mortal danger in an airplane. The devil was lying in wait for you. But you were protected by the Lord." The man he warned replied: "I am actually planning to fly to London and Ireland. Please pray for my flight."

   Six weeks later the man who had been warned was sitting in an airplane. The weather was clear over England. As soon as they were flying over the sea, a terrible storm set in.

   During its landing in Ireland, the plane had to make a second approach. During the second landing attempt, it veered suddenly to the right, then to the left, and came to a stop standing on its head. In spite of this, no one was injured.

As a result of the warning at the missionary conference, the family of the traveling missionary and his brethren from the conference had been praying for his safety.

3. A third form of prophetic insight in the present is the unconscious inspiration of someone who preaches the gospel. Every devout evangelist, missionary, or pastor has at one time or another had the experience in the course of his preaching of saying something unconsciously that moved the conscience of a listener.

Earlier, when my friend and pastor Gottlieb Weiland was still alive, I often had such an experience during his preaching. Once in the church of a village in the Black Forest he told a story about a teacher. Afterward the organist, a teacher by profession, came to me quite upset and said, "What made your friend tell that story about me in the church in front of everyone?" I went to see my friend in the sacristy and asked him, "Gottlieb, where did you get that story about the teacher? There is a teacher outside who says you told a story about him." Gottlieb replied, "During my sermon this story occurred to me as a parable, not as a true experience." And yet it had been the story of the organist.

4. All preaching that is inspired by God can be the gift of prophecy. All true proclamation of the Word that is guided by the Spirit is a bit of prophecy that touches the conscience of the listeners.

8. Discernment of spirits (diakriseis pneumaton)

With this gift of the Spirit we come to an extremely

111

distressing area. The Greek word for devil, *diabolos,* means "sower of confusion." In actual fact the intellectual and spiritual movements of our day are becoming increasingly confused.

The Enemy is especially cunning in mixing lies with truth. The admixture of biblical motifs is a tempting bait for the faithful. Here we see fulfilled II Corinthians 11:14, a passage that must be quoted frequently today: "Satan himself is transformed into an angel of light."

Of all the gifts of the Spirit, I find it most necessary to pray for the gift of discernment of spirits, because my particular ministry demands it. For years I have been receiving inquiries from all over the world: What do you think of transcendental meditation? What do you think about eye diagnosis and acupuncture? What do you think about Jakob Lorber? Where should Oral Roberts, Tommy Hicks, Osborn, Wilkerson, Kathryn Kuhlman be classified? How can those who are mentally ill or hysterical be distinguished from those who are possessed? May we make use of the healing powers of the spiritualist Harry Edwards and of magicians? What do you think about the movie *The Exorcist*?

This type of problem led me to write books about these questions and to pray without ceasing for the gift of discernment of spirits. I would be horrified at the prospect of launching a critical attack on children of God who have genuine spiritual powers.

Before we cast some light on the question of discernment of spirits, the role of the human intellect must first be clarified.

In the book by Mel Tari, for example, we read: "We want to send the tiny computer we have in our brain to the moon and in faith trust totally in the Lord.''

This statement is well intended; in a particular instance it might be said to a hardened rationalist. Generally speaking, however, such counsel is in error. God gave us our intellects to develop and to use.

Paul gives the following advice in I Corinthians 14:20: ''Brethren, be not children in understanding: howbeit in malice be ye children, but in understanding be men.''

In I Thess. 5:21 likewise he counsels men to use their intellects, saying, ''Prove all things.''

The apostle John writes in the same vein in I John 4:1: ''Beloved, believe not every spirit, but try the spirits whether they are of God: because many false prophets are gone out into the world.''

The passages from Scripture tell us that we should strive to receive the best education possible. To pray for the Holy Spirit with His power and authority does not rule out the activity of the intellect, but rather implies it.

Thus anyone whose pastoral work involves the sick or even the possessed should have, if at all possible, medical training. We must be in a position to distinguish mental illness, spiritual trouble, and demonic possession. Misdiagnosis can lead to disaster.

While I write this, the mailman is once more leaving a pile of letters on my desk. One involves a pastoral problem. A woman tells how an untrained pastor told her she was possessed. To judge from her account, that is simply untrue. I have been working for decades in this dangerous area and can recognize genuine instances of possession. But I have never told anyone that he was possessed. Nor will I ever do so, because I consider that a dangerous course. Such a statement places an added burden on anyone who comes for counseling, sick and burdened already.

All these points argue that we should draw as much as possible on the intellects our creator has given us.

And yet even with the best education, no human intellect is sufficient to make judgments in spiritual matters. Paul states: "But the natural man receiveth not the things of the Spirit of God. . . .But he that is spiritual judgeth all things" (I Cor. 2:14-15).

Many psychiatrists have not been reborn and therefore are not endowed with the Holy Spirit; therefore they see people who are possessed by demons and call them hysterical or mentally ill, and begin an erroneous course of therapy.

There are erroneous diagnoses on both sides. Both psychiatrists and theologians can be wrong. Therefore we need alongside the best possible scientific education the gift of the Holy Spirit in order to be able to judge the chaotic movements of our day.

Some time ago a preacher thought he would make me happy by sending me the prophecies of a "new prophetess," Berta Dudde. I received a total of three booklets. They contain direct dialogue between Jesus and Berta Dudde on the subject of Jesus' return. I read a few pages and wrote back to the preacher asking him not to send me any more. These dialogues are permeated with religious spiritualism; they are reminiscent of Jakob Lorber in Europe and Edgar Cayce in North America.

At present the healing assemblies of Kathryn

Kuhlman present a problem that is simply insoluble. I have letters of enthusiastic approval and letters of violent repudiation. Kathryn Kuhlman belongs to the charismatic movement, which I cannot go along with. I was only surprised that the harshest criticism came from the ranks of the charismatic movement. Kathryn Kuhlman was at the Jerusalem Congress in April 1974, and spoke there. Men and women from the Pentecostal churches took serious exception to her. I do not want to discuss the subject further in this context.

One fact contributes most to the confusion of the faithful. There are preachers and simple children of God who boast in the cross of Jesus, His death, His resurrection and ascension, and yet say at the same time: "We have to have more than this. We have to achieve perfection, full salvation—and that happens when we have the gift of tongues as a demonstration of baptism in the Spirit." This is false doctrine. Jesus and what He did are sufficient. We need nothing more.

This brings us to the most controversial gift of the Spirit.

9. Speaking in tongues (glossa)

Before entering this highly controversial area, I want to say at the outset that I, too, believe in this gift of the Holy Spirit. Whatever may be said in this chapter does not effect the true gift. Therefore anyone who has received from the Holy Spirit the gift of worshiping in an alien tongue need not be upset. I know and take to heart the words of Psalm 105:15:

"Touch not mine anointed, and do my prophets no harm."

Within this brief compass the whole problem of glossolalia cannot be discussed in detail. This I have already done in my booklet *Strife of Tongues*, published also in German and French.

In theological discussion today the gift of tongues is caught between two extremes, as has already been shown.

There are theologians who state that this gift existed only in the first century. Although I am familiar with the unique character of the apostolic age and the power of its miracles, I do not share the view that this gift has fully ceased.

The other extreme is the heretical statement that every Christian who has experienced rebirth must go on to achieve this gift. This position, too, I reject, because it is unbiblical. Jesus did not speak in tongues. The three thousand who came to believe on the first Pentecost did not speak in tongues. And Paul says in I Corinthians 12:30: "Do all speak with tongues? do all interpret?" The apostle's answer is no, because believers do not all have the same gifts.

Holy respect to this gift, an American man of God coined the phrase: "Forbid not, seek not."

Let us first list the New Testament passages that mention glossolalia. They are Mark 16:17; Acts 2; Acts 8:17; Acts 10:46; Acts 19:6; I Corinthians 12—14.

A few words on these texts. Mark 16:17 reads: "And these signs shall follow them that believe; In my name shall they cast out devils; They shall speak with new tongues." The text of Mark is a source of uncertainty for theologians. The earlier manu-

116

scripts, such as Codex Sinaiticus (4th century) and Codex Vaticanus (same period), do not contain Mark 16:9-20. Many minuscule manuscripts likewise do not exhibit this conclusion to Mark. On the other hand, later codices like Codex Ephraemi (5th century) and Codex Bezae Cantabrigiensis (6th century) contain this conclusion to Mark.

Personally, this does not bother me at all. I am open to textual studies, but not to textual criticism. Since we have this conclusion to Mark in our Bible, I respect it; it came into being under the guidance of the Holy Spirit, and we must accept this situation with gratitude. The Conclusion to Mark breathes the spirit of all four Gospels.

The events recounted in Acts 2 cannot be looked on as glossolalia. Many theologians, like Dr. Dickason of the Moody Bible Institute, point out that Acts 2 uses the same Greek word, *glossa,* as I Corinthians 12—14. They therefore conclude that the phenomena discussed are the same. This philological conclusion is not convincing, because theological investigation reveals a different situation.

In Acts 2 we have a language miracle. The apostles were able to preach the gospel to the sixteen or seventeen nationalities present in Jerusalem, to each man in his own language. No translator was needed.

In I Corinthians 12—14 we are dealing with glossolalia, a speaking in tongues not understood by anyone, often not even by the person speaking. In this case a translator or interpreter was necessary.

In Acts 2 we are dealing with missionary preaching of the gospel. In the Epistle to the Corinthians, we are dealing with prayer in alien tongues, with worship, with the praise of God.

Acts 8:14-17 relates the journey of Peter and John to Samaria. There they met believers who had not yet heard about the outpouring of the Holy Spirit. Therefore the apostles informed them and laid hands on them, and they received the Holy Spirit. That is not our situation. We have Pentecost with the outpouring of the Holy Spirit behind us. The people of Samaria had two steps in their spiritual development: first they accepted Christ as their Savior; then later on they experienced the baptism in the Holy Spirit. We Christians have two events in one experience. We receive the Holy Spirit along with the new birth. Recall the word: "nobody can say that Jesus is the Lord, but by the Holy Spirit" (I Cor. 12:3).

Acts 10 contains the story of the Roman centurion Cornelius, who was filled with the Spirit of God and given the gift of tongues after he accepted salvation. The point of this story is to demonstrate to the Jewish Christians that the Gentiles are called to the same salvation. Since Peter states in Act 10:47: "Can any man forbid water, that these should not be baptized, which have received the Holy Spirit *as well as we?*" we may assume that this passage does not refer to glossolalia, but to an event like that recounted in Acts 2.

Acts 19 records Paul's arrival in Ephesus. The apostle noted that there was something wrong with these Christians. Therefore he asked them, "Have ye received the Holy Spirit since ye believed?" (v. 2). They proved to be ignorant, because they had heard only the preaching of Apollos. When Paul prayed with them and laid his hands on them, the Holy Spirit came on them. They spoke in tongues and prophesied. The word "prophesied," introduced by translators, is an unfortunate choice. The Greek original here reads *epropheteuon*, which means "they spoke prophetically." This means that we are not dealing here with glossolalia, but with the same phenomenon as that in Acts 2 and 10. In addition, this passage must not be misused, as it often is by extremist groups. The Ephesians represent a transitional situation. They are on a course of development that leads from paganism through the baptism of repentance preached by John to the receiving of the Holy Spirit. We must not turn this into a doctrine of stages. The Ephesians knew nothing of Pentecost. We know Pentecost and have it behind us.

All the passages in Acts speak not of glossolalia but of prophetic speaking in a foreign language, which could be understood without an interpreter.

The situation in the Epistle to the Corinthians is different. Here we are no longer dealing with a language miracle. Three forms of speaking in tongues can be distinguished in I Corinthians 14:

1. I Cor. 14:2: "He that speaketh in an unknown tongue speaketh not unto men, but unto God." This is a gift given for the worship of God and the glorification of His mysteries. (See also I Cor. 14:4, 28.)
2. I Cor. 14:5: "Greater is he that prophesieth than he that speaketh with tongues, except he interpret, that the church may receive edifying."
3. I Cor. 14:22, 21: " Tongues are for a sign, not to them that believe, but to them that believe not; and yet for all that will they not hear me."

It can be a sign of judgment and of hardening of hearts for the unbelievers. Paul finds positive things to say about speaking in tongues:

1. I Cor. 14:18: "I speak with tongues more than ye all."
2. I Cor. 14:39: "Forbid not to speak with tongues."

Since the gift of tongues created much disorder and confusion in Corinth, the apostle sets out rules for the use of the gift of tongues:

1. I Cor. 14:19: Better five words with understanding than ten thousand in tongues.
2. V. 27: Only two or at most three to speak in tongues.
3. V. 27: One at a time.
4. V. 28: No speaking in tongues without an interpreter.
5. V. 32: The gift of tongues must be subject to control.
6. V. 33: Speaking in tongues must not produce confusion.
7. V. 40: Speaking in tongues must be done decently and in order.
8. V. 34: Women must not speak in tongues publicly in church (note the context).

Since this saying in verse 34 has been frequently misinterpreted, a brief explanation must be given. The New Testament gives some regulations with respect to women.

The ministry of women is restricted

1. *I Cor. 14:34: Women are not to speak in tongues in church.*

2. *I Tim. 2:12: Women may not exercise a teaching office. ("I suffer not a woman to teach.")*

The ministry of women is permitted

1. I Cor. 11:5: Women may pray and prophesy in church.
2. Acts 21:9: The four daughters of the evangelist Philip prophesy.
3. Acts 16:14-15: Women have a ministry of service.

The tongues movement today

Although I support the biblical gift of tongues, I have said a firm no to the so-called tongues movement. Why? The eight points made by Paul in the Epistle to the Corinthians are neither observed nor obeyed. Most of those who pray in tongues are women; no interpreter is present; there are sometimes twenty women or more; occasionally they even pray simultaneously; in the extremist groups things are not done decently and in order; finally, they turn the gift into a law and make it the criterion of baptism in the Spirit.

In the tongues movement, the devil has succeeded in making giant inroads into the church of Jesus.

My most recent example should be mentioned. It comes from Prince Edward Island, one of the eastern provinces of Canada.

A devout pastor was holding a weekly prayer meeting. Present were the pastor, his wife, and some believers belonging to the congregation. In the midst of the prayer meeting the wife suddenly began to pray in tongues. The pastor was horrified. This was the first time it had happened in his congregation. Hardly had she finished when another woman who was a believer began to speak in tongues. There was no interpreter. The pastor felt uneasy. He broke off the prayer meeting and sent the members home.

As I see it, the wife has allowed herself to be tainted. She owns a large number of fetishes, idols, devil masks, and all kinds of cultic objects from the mission field. She thinks of herself as a collector of harmless objects, not realizing that a person can be tainted by cultic objects that have served for devil worship. Other Christians have the same impression. They, too, think this woman is tainted. It is a common experience for people to speak in tongues in the vicinity of an occult taint or mediumistic capabilities, or even in the train of spiritualism.

Meanwhile, this "irruption of tongues" in the prayer meeting ended in tragedy. The pastor's wife and the second woman who spoke in tongues both lost their minds and are in a mental hospital.

To the gifts of the Holy Spirit, an unqualified yes. The prophecy concerning the eschaton (second coming of the Lord, etc.) is finished with the canon (collection of the N.T.). Some other gifts play an important role only for a limited period—without having totally ceased—while others will continue to be relevant until the return of Jesus.

To all gifts that are the product of demonic inspiration or even of human aping, a radical, a firm no.

Finally, let me give some remarks concerning tongues:

1. The Epistle to the Corinthians was written in the spring of 57 A.D. The later epistles of the apos-

tles do not have the problem of tongues. We see by this fact that the tongues were already diminishing.

2. The Corinthian congregation was the most troublesome and carnal congregation of the apostle Paul. In the mature congregations there was no problem of tongues.
3. For centuries of church history, there was no "strife of tongues."
4. Who makes a law out of tongues is a heretic.
5. The Bible contains all we need for our salvation.
6. It would be a blessing and a gift of the Holy Spirit if our own tongue would be liberated from all evil speaking and sanctified for the adoration of God.

10. Interpretation of tongues (ermeneia glosson)

It is always refreshing to find occasional positive examples. In one place where there was a revival among the illiterate population, I was witness to a genuine language miracle.

On another occasion I was impressed by a fluent prayer in a strange tongue, rich in vowels. The interpretation was equally fluent, and was a triumphant paean of praise for the victory of Jesus throughout the world.

I look back on these two examples with gratitude.

With respect to the interpretation of tongues, however, I have had more negative than positive experiences.

A missionary from Africa was spending his furlough in Europe. He was visiting the prayer meeting of a pentecostal church when suddenly he heard a prayer in the African dialect that he himself knew. The prayer consisted of all kinds of blasphemies against the Holy Trinity. The missionary left the room so as not to share responsibility for the offense. He waited outside until the meeting was over and told the astonished speaker what he had been praying.

Here we are not dealing with interpretation through a gift of the Holy Spirit, but rather with interpretation through knowledge of a studied language. It is therefore not an example of the gift of interpretation.

A different experience casts no more light on this problem. A converted Jewish Christian was praying the first Psalm in Hebrew. Another participant, who did not know any Hebrew, stood up and gave the "interpretation." The Hebraist was shocked. He told the "interpreter": "Your interpretation was wrong. It was Psalm 1 in the original language of the Bible."

With respect to interpretation I am groping in the dark. I myself have never had this gift, nor have I been able to substantiate the accuracy of any interpretations.

The fact remains that there is a gift of interpretation, which was certainly abundantly present in the apostolic age but has now gone into a marked eclipse. Interpretation is only a supplementary gift to the gift of tongues.

11. Apostles (apostoloi) (I Cor. 12:28-30)

In I Corinthians 12, the end of the chapter provides a second and a third list of the gifts of the Spirit. We will examine those gifts not already mentioned at the beginning of the chapter.

By "apostles" in the strict sense we mean the men called to this office as eyewitnesses by Jesus Himself. The word derives from the Greek word *apostolos*, which means ambassador.

These ambassadors and messengers called by Jesus were equipped with threefold authority for their ministry (Luke 9:1-2):

Authority to preach,

Authority to heal the sick, and

Authority to drive out demons.

On the question of authority, many critical voices have been raised. They say: Preaching is a question of theological education. Healing the sick is a job for doctors. Driving out demons is out of date, for what the age of Jesus called possession was only mental illness. Today that is the domain of psychiatrists.

From beginning to end, these arguments contain illogic, ignorance, and inexperience.

The best of rhetoric, the most brilliant words from the pulpit do not constitute authority, which only the Holy Spirit can give.

Divine healing lies on a different plane than medical treatment.

To look on possession as mental illness is a fatal mistake reserved to our unbelieving psychiatrists and modern theologians. The New Testament itself distinguishes the sick from the demoniacs. This can be seen in Matthew 4:24; 8:16; 10:1; Mark 1:32. Or consider only the passage mentioned above, Luke 9:1-2. Healing is distinguished from driving out demons. Jesus and His disciples were not a group of backward rustics, as unregenerate scholars would have us believe.

What the apostles received from their Lord they passed on to others:

"And they went forth, and preached every where, the Lord working with them, and confirming the word with signs following" (Mark 16:20);

"And God wrought special miracles by the hands of Paul"(Acts 19:11).

Besides the inner circle of disciples, other messengers of Jesus in the New Testament are given the name "apostles,"for example, Barnabas in Acts 14:14 and Epaphroditus in Philippians 2:25 (in the Greek original). This naturally refers only to their missionary ministry, not their direct, personal call on the part of Jesus.

In the history of Christian missions, men of God who have been especially blessed have been honored with the epithet "apostle." In Flachsmeier's history of evangelical world missions, for example, we find the following:

Ansgar, Apostle of the North (801-865) (p.57)

Constantine and Methodius, Apostles of the Slavs (815-885) (p. 62)

Otto von Bamberg, Apostle of Pommerania (1060-1139) (p. 66)

Hans Egede, Apostle of the Eskimos (1686-1758) (p. 135)

Robert Morrison, Apostle of China (1782-1839) (p. 202)

Adoniram Judson, Apostle of Burma (1788-1850) (p. 212)

As is the case with all gifts of the Spirit, there are also false representatives of all offices:

Rev. 2:2: "Which say they are apostles, and are not."

II Cor. 11:13: "For such are false apostles, . . .

transforming themselves into the apostles of Christ."

Matt. 7:15: "Beware of false prophets."

I John 4:1: "many false prophets are gone out."

Matt. 24:24; "There shall arise false Christs, and false prophets."

II Cor. 11:26: "In perils among false brethren."

The experience of having to suffer much among false brethren was not limited to the apostle Paul. Even now it is the order of the day. My discussion of Indonesia has given some examples.

It should be mentioned that many sects today also give their leaders the title "apostle," without having the least justification. It is not just pious fantasy but the product of a lying spirit for the New Apostolic Church to consider its leading apostles the direct successors of the apostles of Jesus.

It is by the direct inspiration of Satan that men even come forward today claiming to be Christ returned. More than ten such deceivers are attempting to make an impact on the various continents. My most recent experience of this sort comes from my last tour in the United States. A sixteen-year-old youth from India, who holds assemblies with meditation and yoga, gives himself out to be the Lord returned. And even he finds his disciples and followers.

12. Teachers (didaskoloi) (I Cor. 12:28)

When the apostle Paul speaks of teachers in the passage in Corinthians, he naturally is not referring to the instructional staff of our schools.

In both Europe and North America we have Communist teachers who poison the souls of the children with their atheism.

I once read in an American church paper that in the United States a list was published containing the names of six thousand teachers who are avowed Communists.

I am also acquainted with a protest written by Billy Graham with the statement that believing parents are unwilling to let their children be contaminated by atheists in the public schools.

In the European countries, where there is still religious instruction in the public schools, there are other problems involving teachers of religion who are modernists. Believing parents who join with their children at home in reading the Bible, in prayer, and in having respect for the Word of God, have to live through having their children come back from religious instruction and report the devastation being wrought by the religion instructors at school. I once went so far as to advise my daughter: "Withdraw from the religion class. I do not want to see you exposed to these poisonous vapors." She did not do as I suggested, for fear of the consequences.

If a school teacher is a reborn Christian, he is a teacher by the grace of God who may reach out through faith and prayer for a gift of teaching bestowed by the Holy Spirit. For the Holy Spirit leads into all truth, reveals the meaning of Scripture, and equips men to exercise the teaching office. And there have been thousands of such teachers in the history of the church and its mission. But the Holy Spirit does not patronize laziness. He does not do for us what we can do ourselves.

When Paul referred to the teaching ability given by the Spirit, he was of course thinking primarily of the Bible teachers who instruct the church of Jesus and its young people.

In the United States and Canada we find the admirable practice of having Sunday school before the main worship service, not only for children but also for adults. In this respect we Europeans are too conceited, and reject Sunday school for adults as "childish nonsense." We are wrong. The Sunday schools of North America have helped to produce many missionaries.

I will mention only one example. At the First Presbyterian Church of Hollywood, Miss Henrietta Mears built up an elaborate Sunday school program. She began during the thirties with a group of difficult girls who called themselves snobs. After just a few weeks, a hundred girls were coming to her Sunday school. After three decades, there were sixty-five hundred enrolled in the Sunday school of this church. Each week Miss Mears had to prepare five hundred teachers for the individual classes. In the course of her blessed ministry as a Sunday school teacher, more than six hundred young people decided to become missionaries. When Billy Graham was once asked what woman had most influenced him spiritually, he replied, "Except for my wife and my mother, it was Miss Mears who had the greatest spiritual influence on my life."

I met Miss Mears in 1962, when I delivered a series of lectures at the First Presbyterian Church of Hollywood. The story of her life will be found beginning on page 364 of my book *Unter der Fuhrung Jesu.*

In Germany, too, there have been teachers filled

with the Spirit. My revered teacher Prof. Karl Heim of the University of Tubingen has already been mentioned. I also want to mention Erich Sauer, a Bible teacher at the Wiedenest Bible school. His books have been translated into English.

There are also many Bible teachers in the United States and Canada who are equipped by the Holy Spirit. We find such teachers at Moody Bible Institute, Wheaton College, Biola, Bob Jones University, and at many other institutions of learning.

The Lord has fashioned Himself many instruments, not all of whom can be mentioned in this book. Their glory belongs to the Man on the cross who redeemed them and equipped them for the special ministry that the Lord has entrusted to them.

13. Helps (antilempsis) (I Cor. 12:28)

The Greek word *antilempsis* used by Paul means, among other things, assistance, help.

Helpers are much in demand but are hard to find. An English woman who was traveling in Germany with her husband was standing beside the freeway, trying to attract attention. Her car was off on the shoulder. Her husband was lying unconscious in the car, the victim of a heart attack. She stood there for two hours. Finally, after three hours, she got her husband to the hospital. But he died on the way. He could have been saved, the doctors said, if he had received a shot to support his circulation during the first half hour.

In service to the church of Jesus many helpers are necessary. The church is not a one-man show. But how few are ready to serve.

In Canada I was addressing a Baptist congregation. As in many churches, the pastor had to perform all the ministries of his church himself. His wife plays the organ. On weekdays he cleans the church. He takes care of the office work alone. He is an overworked man, and always looks exhausted. Would that be necessary if there were helpers in his congregation who had the gift of helping?

I am writing this chapter under trying circumstances. Five days ago my wife had a serious operation. Everything went well, but three days later she began to run a high fever and have severe pain. The doctors are talking about an infection of unknown origin. How good it is that—besides Him who is the great help in time of need—I have several friends who regularly receive my circular letters whom I could call up or inform by mail. In the kingdom of God, helpers in prayer are the most important helpers. They often stand in the background unrecognized. They usually do not serve with important titles and positions, and yet they do a decisive ministry—indeed the most important of all; they approach the throne of God to help others.

At this point I must recall that this book is dedicated to all the people who receive my circular letters. I have been put to shame by many believers whom I do not even know. I had discontinued sending to my old mailing list, because many addresses had changed (as well as for other reasons.) I thought 5 or 10 percent would get in contact with me. How surprised I was when more than two-thirds wanted to continue receiving the letters!

I have also received other help. Some of the faithful in Germany and Switzerland take care of the mailings. Others help me with the office work. My wife packed hundreds of shipments of books for the Scripture mission and will continue to do so if she is allowed to return from the hospital restored to health. A retired woman in Hamburg copies my manuscripts and takes care of much of my pastoral correspondence. These are helpers who selflessly take over when my waning strength no longer suffices. How grateful I am, and I thank with all my heart those whose hands are occupied with help and prayer.

"Help" is hardly recognized as a gift of the Spirit. And yet we must hear the message: the help given by hearts filled with the Spirit differs from that given by social activists. What matters is the motive. Two men may do the same thing, but it is not really the same thing. This fact is long familiar to Christians.

14. Governors (kybernesis) (I Cor. 12:28)

The Greek word *kybernesis,* from which we derive the word *cybernetics,* means guidance, leadership, governance. It would be hard to imagine our politicians receiving their office to govern from the hand of God. Election campaigns are often fought with every means at the candidates' disposal. We have only to think of the Watergate scandal or the assassination of political opponents. Politics is a dirty business, involving money, intrigue, tricks, quackery, and bitter struggles for power.

And yet there have been politicians who were also believers. One or two presidents of the United States in the past century are noted for having been faithful Christians. Believers have also sat on the throne of

England. In Canada, Ernest Manning, who was the Premier of Alberta for twenty years, was an active Christian who happily bore witness to his faith. In 1966 he passed the word by radio for all Christians in Canada to pray for a revival. I should also mention Robert Thompson, living now at Fort Langley, British Columbia, who years ago was the leader of the Conservative Party in British Columbia. He is a man of prayer.

In East Asia, Syngman Rhee should be mentioned. When he was fighting in the Resistance against the Japanese, he was arrested and thrown into prison. There he was converted. At first he evangelized his fellow prisoners. After the Japanese left, he was set free and became the first president of South Korea. He has won many for Jesus. It is unusual for a former Resistance fighter and president to live the life of a consistent Christian.

In the church sector, there have been bishops and other leaders who have brought disaster on the Christian community. We need only think, for example, of the spiritualist Bishop Pike or Bishop Robinson, the English churchman whose book *Honest to God* showed that he was a modernist. Modern theology is the very opposite of following Jesus.

Of course we also have bishops who have surrendered their lives to Jesus and receive their responsible office afresh each day from the hands of the Lord. I will mention only one, the unforgettable Bavarian bishop Hermann Bezzel.

When I was lecturing to the Eclectic Society in England, my friend Richard Bewes told me that in England they have a bishop who is a believer and strongly supports the evangelicals.

Most leaders who are filled with the Spirit and devote their lives to God are found in the history of the church and its mission. The reformers, whose lives have been extolled by hundreds of authors, are examples.

From the missionary field I will mention a single man, whose example stands for many: Hudson Taylor. In the book *Hudson Taylor's Spiritual Secret* (Moody Press), the Foreword states: "He was a man gifted with a remarkable talent for organization, with energetic initiative, with tireless endurance, and an amazing influence on men. At the same time, he had a childlike humility. Truly, Hudson Taylor was God's chosen instrument."

It is possible to govern the nation or the church with a natural talent and an innate organizational ability. But it is also possible to govern with a wisdom and a gift bestowed by the Spirit of God. Lest the fact be forgotten, it will be repeated once more: the Holy Spirit can also purify, sanctify, and use a natural talent.

15. Love (agape) (I Cor. 13)

Between the two chapters on the gifts of the Spirit, the apostle constructs his paean to love.

The Greek language has richer resources than English for talking about love. The Greeks distinguish *eros, philia,* and *agape.*

During the fifth and fourth centuries before Christ, *eros* at first did not mean sexual love. It was an esthetic love, which later also came to be called Platonic love. The meaning of the word soon changed, however. By the time of Jesus, *eros* was already understood as sexual love.

Philia is love for one's family and friends. While the word *eros* does not appear in the New Testament, the word *philia* occurs twenty-five times.

When love is mentioned among the gifts of the Spirit, what is meant is *agape*. This term appears 250 times in the New Testament as a noun or adjective.

It is not by chance that love stands in the midst of the gifts of the Spirit and is also listed as one of the fruits of the Spirit in Galatians 5:22. Love is both a fruit and a gift. In Romans 5:5, Paul says, "The love of God is shed abroad in our hearts by the Holy Spirit."

All the extreme groups who rank the gift of tongues above all else must be told on the basis of I Corinthians 13 that the gift of tongues, as well as all wisdom and knowledge, all healing powers and miracles, is nothing without love.

The word "love" is often misunderstood. It has nothing to do with sweet weakness and false politeness. It has been said that love without truth is not love. Conversely, truth without love is not truth.

I have traveled extensively among the English-speaking nations. There is an obvious difference between them and the Germans. The English speaking world places more value on politeness than does the German-speaking world. This has its advantages and its disadvantages. A man who is polite has an easier time of it. The disadvantage is that the man who is polite has to make more compromises. Now I must record some of my own observations. For reasons of politeness, false doctrines are much more easily swallowed in England, the United States, Australia, and Canada than elsewhere. No one dares dispute false doctrine. This readiness to compromise, this indulgence and politeness are censured by the exalted Lord in Revelation 2—3. "But I have a few things against thee, because thou hast there them that hold the doctrine of Balaam" (Rev. 2:14); "I have a few things against thee, because thou sufferest that woman Jezebel, which calleth herself a prophetess, to teach and to seduce. . . ." (Rev. 2:20).

Heretics are allowed to spread their false doctrines, and out of politeness no one resists them. Of course we do not burn people at the stake, but false doctrine should be publicly condemned from the pulpit. That is no offense against love. On the contrary, preaching of false doctrine wrongs the unsophisticated members of the congregation, who in their ignorance fall victim to such false doctrines.

Truth with love, love with truth!

But let us go on to concrete practice. During one of my tours in India I had a conversation with a high-ranking Indian. We talked about missionary assistance sent by the West. He stated: "Misssionary work has for the most been reduced to social and charitable work. What matters is no longer the salvation of souls, but the building of hospitals, schools, and so forth. This material aid is important, but it is not essential. Hindus and Buddhists can build hospitals, but they cannot bring men to Jesus."

This conversation showed me that the changing values of the Christian churches of the West are already felt in the missionary field. Philanthropic concern for men's bodies is also a part of the gospel, but it is a problem of secondary importance.

136

This brings us to the salient point. Formerly German theology took the field against the social gospel. Today our own theology has reached this point.

"To put the gospel into practice means to be socially engaged." That is one of the watchwords that sounds fine but is out of line with the New Testament.

If our hearts are filled with the love of Jesus, our hands will move automatically. I quote Luther: "Faith does not ask what there is to be done, but is always busily at work."

Anyone who writes about love can only do so with a bad conscience. Who has not offended against love? This consideration alone shows that we have no claim on eternity. What have we to offer with all our gifts if the very foundation, "the love that presses us forward," is not in order?

We have examples of love, beginning with Jesus, who let Himself be nailed to the cross for our sakes. We may think of Tabitha (Acts 9:36-37), who made clothes for the poor without accepting payment. Francis of Assisi stands before us. Mathilde Wrede, the angel of those in prison. George Muller with his ten thousand orphans. Kagawa, the brother of wretched outcasts, in Japan. It would be a long list if we set out to name all the disciples of Jesus who have offered up their lives for others in the Spirit and in love for their Lord. Are we on this list?

16. Ministry (diakonia) (Rom. 12:7)

Now we leave the list of the gifts of the Spirit found in Corinthians and turn our attention to Romans 12. From this text we will single out only those gifts that have not been discussed previously.

The King James version uses the term "ministry." The Greek text contains the word *diakonia*. This brings us to a topic that is the subject of much discussion at present.

The nursing orders are having terrible problems finding young girls who are willing to enter this life. Young men and women are not ready to serve, to minister. To many, a life of freedom and a high standard of living are more important than the way of obedience and service.

This ministry has other problems as well. I have had talks with many deaconesses (as the members of the Protestant nursing orders are called in Germany) who have had to suffer immeasurably under power-hungry superiors. It is not only bureaucrats who love red tape and power structures; the same is true in ecclesiastical circles.

Diaconal ministry is related to the gift of helping. We can therefore summarize briefly at this point.

The great prototype of all who serve, with or without distinctive costume, with or without official position, is Stephen. Scripture calls him "a man full of faith and of the Holy Spirit" (Acts 6:5).

That is ministry, born of the Holy Spirit and bearing the authority of the Holy Spirit. Of the same man is said: "Stephen, full of faith and power, did great wonders and miracles" (Acts 6:8).

Naturally the important thing is not whether we are distinguished by our great wonders and miracles. Hidden service without recognition, performed for the sake of Jesus, is equally important in the eyes of God.

A ministry that we all can share will be suggested in the form of an example. When Louis Harms died, those who placed him in his coffin found that his knees were like leather. Leather knees—how did they come about? Louis Harms spent several hours in prayer every morning. Therefore the Lord used him to found the Hermannsburg mission in Germany and to save many. The faithful with leather knees are the best ministers in the kingdom of God, for intercession is the best ministry God's children can be engaged in.

17. Exhortation (paraklesis) (Rom. 12:8)

The Greek word for exhortation or admonition, *paraklesis* has a wider range of meanings than the English terms. *Parakaleo* means to summon, to call on for help, to exhort, to encourage, to comfort, to strengthen. The noun *paraklesis* therefore has secondary meanings such as exhortation, comfort, encouragement, pastoral care.

The Bible contains wonderful passages of exhortation. Consider, for instance, the farewell of Paul to the elders of the church at Ephesus:

"Take heed therefore unto yourselves, and to all the flock, over the which the Holy Spirit hath made you overseers, to feed the church of God, which he hath purchased with his own blood" (Acts 20:28).

The apostle Paul was a master of exhortation. Consider the Epistle to Philemon. One of my revered teachers, Prof. Martin Schlunk, told us in his Bible course: "The Epistle to Philemon is a masterpiece of exhortation and pastoral care."

Exhortation can be the product of legalism, or it can flow from a heart full of love and understanding. I have experienced both.

There are some of the older brethren so possessed by a tyrannical and pharisaic legalism that they make life difficult for everyone around them. Many women have become spiritually broken under the pious tyranny of their husbands. I have heard confessions of this sort.

I could personally tell many a tale about the havoc wrought in the kingdom of God by legalistic brethren. Great men have not been immune to this failing. Think of John Calvin, under whose influence the physician Michael Servetus died at the stake because he could not believe in the Trinity.

Of course we abhor such unbiblical legalism. It is the approach of the Old Testament. We cannot put men to death because they are unable to believe. On this point we are probably all agreed.

What are we to think, however, when this Calvinistic legalism comes back to life in the United States and Canada? I could cite examples having to do with great men of God out of my own personal experience, but am unwilling to expose them.

Without naming names and places, let me give a brief account. It was in Canada, in the fall of 1974. I was on a lecture tour with my friend Gottfried Amend. At a Bible college in New Brunswick the director gave us the following example: A young man applied to the school. During his interview, the director heard that he had been divorced *before* his conversion. His application was thereupon rejected. That is law, not gospel.

Another example was told my friend by Jack

Wyrtzen. He stated that he had a devout friend who espoused the opinion that no one should remarry after the death of a spouse. Once again, that is legalism, and also unbiblical.

There is also an exhortation based on love. The law strikes out men and injures them. The gospel comforts, binds up wounds, heals.

Another word associated with the Greek words *parakaleo* and *paraklesis* is the noun *parakletos*. And that is the term Jesus uses for the Holy Spirit in His farewell discourses. We find it in John 14—15: "And I will pray the Father, and he shall give you another Comforter, that he may abide with you for ever" (John 14:16); "But when the Comforter is come, . . . he shall testify of me"(John 15:26).

Notwithstanding all the wonderful comfort that believers can bring us, one truth remains inviolate: there is nothing comparable to what the Holy Spirit does for us and there is no one comparable to Him.

> Phil. 1:19: The Holy Spirit "supplies" us with what we need.
> John 6:63: The Holy Spirit brings the Word to life for us.
> John 16:14: The Holy Spirit glorifies Jesus for us.
> Rom. 8:26: The Holy Spirit represents us before God's throne with unutterable groanings.
> John 14—16: The Holy Spirit gives us the encouragement, the assistance, the pastoral care that we need.

Whoever has the Holy Spirit to exhort, to admonish, and to comfort is sent to do the same for others.

18. Giving in simplicity (metadidomi) (Rom. 12:8)

The translators of the Authorized Version rendered Romans 12:8 as follows: "He that giveth, let him do it with simplicity." The word "simplicity" is hard for us to understand today. The translators mean he should give without reflection, without pride in his own actions, with sincerity. This is the sense in which we may take the Greek phrase *metadidomi en aplotei*.

It may seem surprising that generosity should be a gift of the Spirit. But we must accept the context as it stands. In Romans 12:6-9, readiness to make sacrifices is included among the gifts of the Spirit. We therefore accept it as such.

In the forty years of ministry as an evangelist and missionary, I have experienced all varieties of greed and generosity.

I held some services for an Australian congregation. It was announced that the Sunday offering would go to defray my travel expenses. (My airplane ticket had cost some $3,000.) The Germans who were present contributed generously. Unfortunately I never saw a cent of it. Four months later, when I wrote to the pastor, he responded: "The treasurer stole the money."

That is one side of the coin. Fortunately the Lord has other disciples, too. I recall John Ballantyne, a farmer in England. Since he will not get to read this book, I can mention his name without hesitation. One day he wrote to me saying that he had all my books in English. They had brought him many blessings, and now he wanted to share the blessings. He sent two contributions, each of some two hundred to five hundred dollars, for my Scripture mission.

Never lacking anything! That was the confession of the disciples. It is also my confession. The Lord promised life, life in more abundance— and He kept His promise (John 10:11). I could write a long book about how God provides. But there are people who misunderstand this kind of thing.

I have recounted experiences in which my role was passive. I could recount others in which I played an active role. In such cases there is even greater danger of being misunderstood. Legalistic believers enjoy leveling criticism.

Proverbs 11:24 contains an excellent saying: "There is that scattereth, and yet increaseth; and there is that withholdeth more than is meet, but it tendeth to poverty."

Many of the faithful are also unfamiliar with the blessing recorded in Malachi 3:10: "Bring ye all the tithes into the storehouse, that there may be meat in mine house, and prove me now herewith . . . if I will not open you the windows of heaven, and pour you out a blessing, that there shall not be room enough to receive it."

Paul puts it this way in II Corinthians 9:6: "He which soweth sparingly shall reap also sparingly; and he which soweth bountifully shall reap also bountifully."

This is the experience of all the faithful whom the Lord has set free from greed: the more anyone entrusts to the Lord, the more the Lord opens His hands to us.

To round out this short chapter, an example I experienced in the summer of 1974. A young man

143

who would not give his name informed me that he had read my book about Indonesia. It had led him to send me a thousand dollars for my missionary work. The book also produced a second fruit: he was enrolling in a Swiss Bible college. In the meantime he sent an additional eight hundred dollars for the Bible mission.

19. Mercy (eleeo; eleos) (Rom. 12:8)

A discussion of the gifts of the Spirit might give rise to a misunderstanding. Every Christian is expected to exhibit faith, love, readiness to help, generosity, mercy, and so forth. There can be no discipleship without these traits. But alongside the general features of the Christian life there can be a special gift of the Spirit.

Mercy in this context refers to human relationships. The practice of mercy has its model and roots in the mercy that God shows us.

Ps. 103:8: "The Lord is merciful and gracious";
Luke 1:50: "His mercy is on them that fear him from generation to generation";
Eph. 2:4: "God, who is rich in mercy. . . ."

Because God showed mercy to us sinners, He expects us to show mercy in turn.

Matt. 9:13: "I will have mercy, and not sacrifice";
James 2:13: "he shall have judgment without mercy, that hath showed no mercy."

Sympathy is commonly found today among the faithful. Mercy has become rare.

Someone has reinterpreted the parable of the Samaritan who showed mercy (Luke 10). In the original story, the priest and the Levite passed by the unfortunate victim without noticing his distress.

144

Today things are different. The priest and the Levite pick up clubs and beat the victim to death. Spiritually I have experienced it myself.

What do I want to demonstrate by this parable? There are many famous men of God on both sides of the ocean—well known across the continents—who preach the gospel and practice the Old Testament law. It is questionable if their ministry consists of soul winning or soul killing. They preach love and practice hardness. One of these men wrote to a missionary: "We do not forgive your sin; so the Lord will also not forgive you." That means God has to ask such well-known experts of gospel preaching if He is allowed to forgive sins.

20. Evangelists (euangilisthes) (Eph. 4:11)

Following our examination of I Corinthians 12 and Romans 12, we now turn to Ephesians 4:11. This passage speaks of the ministries of evangelists and pastors. We will first turn our attention to the work of an evangelist.

By way of introduction let me cite a friend's experience. During his vacation, this friend of mine was traveling in Schleswig, Germany. One Sunday morning he heard the bells summoning him to worship. He went to a Lutheran church. The Lutheran pastor welcomed him as the only person there. No—the pastor's wife was also there as organist. After a few words to the effect that there was no point in holding a worship service under these circumstances, the pastor invited my friend to his house for a cup of coffee and a game of chess.

A few years later I heard that several pastors in Schleswig asked their superiors to cancel regular worship services and declare Schleswig a missionary territory. Naturally this suggestion was not approved.

I once had a similar experience myself. A pastor who was not a believer invited me to deliver the Sunday sermon on a special occasion. The only ones who appeared for the service were the organist and an elderly couple. Even the pastor himself wasn't there. Later it occurred to me that possibly they were playing a joke on me. As I later found out, no word of my coming had been mentioned in believing circles; otherwise I would at least have had believers around the pulpit. Since this church had been bled white, I did not conduct any service. There was no singing. I stood in the pew in front of the elderly couple and delivered a biblical message to them. In the forty years of my ministry, only once have I had such an experience. As I have heard, this pastor has now been decorated, either by the state or by the church. That was the story in a church paper.

Today many churches have come to the point where what they need is not a pastor but a missionary or an evangelist. Let us take up the broad problem of *evangelism*. Evangelism is not just the ministry of evangelists, but of all convinced Christians.

The New Testament uses three terms for evangelism: *euangelion* (gospel; Mark 1:1); *euangelizesthai* (evangelize, preach the gospel; Matt. 11:5); *euangelisthes* (evangelist; Eph. 4:11)

a. The term "gospel" in Greek comes originally from military usage and means news of victory. In New Testament usage the meaning changes to "good news." Kittel's *Theological Dictionary of the*

New Testament says, "If one were to summarize the content of the gospel in a single phrase, it would be 'Jesus Christ.' "

b. To evangelize, to preach the gospel, therefore means nothing less than to preach Jesus Christ. A statement of the Anglican Archbishop's Committee on Evangelism states: "To evangelize means to represent Jesus Christ to men through the power of the Holy Spirit, so that they believe in God, accept Jesus as their savior, and worship him as their king in his church." Kittel's *Dictionary* also contains a good definition: "To evangelize means not merely to speak and to preach, but to proclaim with power and authority. Signs and wonders accompany the message of the gospel. They go together, for the Word is effectual. Proclamation of the time of God's grace, of the Kingdom of God, creates a situation that is healthy in all respects. Therefore bodily ills are healed, just as the relationship between man and God is set right." It must be noted that the verb "evangelize" is used in the middle voice in the New Testament; it is semipassive. He who evangelizes does not act on his own authority by virtue of his popular eloquence. Rhetorical technique may stir the soul, but it does not produce rebirth. We cannot lend a helping hand to Christ and the Holy Spirit. The Word of God and the Holy Spirit are the agents. The evangelist is only the commissioned bearer of the good news, the instrument of God.

c. The term "evangelist" occurs only three times in the New Testament: Acts 21:8; Ephesians 4:11; and II Timothy 4:5. It is hard to define the ministry of an evangelist in the New Testament so as to distinguish it from that of others who proclaim Christ. The Bonn theologian Christlieb sees in the office of evangelist an extension of the office of apostle. As conditions for their ministry he suggests personal experience of salvation and constancy in following Jesus. As a specific gift, it demands popular eloquence, grounded in the Bible, stirring and having the power of the Spirit, together with a heart for the spiritual needs of the people. To summarize in three points: we expect of an evangelist a personal communion with Christ; constant attention to the Word of God, interpreted according to a theology that is clearly biblical; and the gift of reviving faith through proclamation of Christ.

d. The purpose of evangelism is to build up the church of Jesus Christ, and in particular to reach those who are far off. The goal is to win men for Jesus and incorporate them into the host of those who are called forth (*ekklesia*). Here Scriver motto applies: souls, souls, and no trivialities. Wichern addressed his famous appeal to Christendom: "A baptism of fire and a baptism of the Spirit must break forth in the church if all this is to take place. In the strength of this baptism the Word will once more go forth, borne by hosts of evangelists. When will this day dawn?" The second section of the Ecumenical Conference at Evanston wrote in its report: "The most important goal of all church work is to aim at revival, conversion, and re-birth."

Although every Christian is called to confess Jesus Christ, evangelistic talent is a distinct gift of the

Holy Spirit. But this gift must not be misused for private purposes, for strange teachings and pet projects.

A brief example. Years ago I received an invitation to lecture at a large church. The pastor in question wanted to build a parish house. He said he needed the offerings from the week of lectures. For this man, therefore, the projected campaign of evangelism was only a fund-raising effort.

21. Pastors (poimen) (Eph. 4:11)

My friend Gottlieb Weiland used to say, "There are shepherds who are more interested in the wool than the weal of the sheep." The ugly word "collection preachers" has been coined for such men. Missionaries and evangelists who worry about the offering are in danger of becoming dependent on the wealthy.

The apostle Peter was aware of this danger of dependence when he wrote: "Feed the flock of God which is among you, taking the oversight thereof, not by constraint, but willingly; not for filthy lucre, but of a ready mind" (I Peter 5:2).

What are the jobs of a shepherd? His duties, by profession, are three: to lead, to provide, and to protect.

To lead. A shepherd goes ahead of his sheep and does not drive them before him. He is always the man out in front.

In terms of spiritual functions in work for the kingdom of God, this can have many meanings. The shepherd of souls should be the great example for his flock—in his prayer life, in readiness to make sacrifices, in study of Scripture, in love, in self-denial, and in many other things. How often, however, the shepherds of souls are put to shame by those entrusted to their care! That is cause for reflection and penance.

To provide. The shepherd has the job of finding proper pastures for his flock. During the Old Testament period there were already many quarrels among shepherds. Today the situation is different. In Europe, pastures are very scarce. There are very few flocks left, and those that exist have difficulty being let in to graze.

Applied to shepherds of souls, this can mean, for instance, that the pastor must see to it that his congregation has biblical nourishment set before it, not false doctrine. Spiritual pastures, too, have grown scarce. What is sometimes served up from the pulpits often cries out to heaven. I could cite many examples. One striking instance may be recorded.

Years ago I met Pastor H.H. Harms of St. Michael's church in Hamburg. I was giving a series of lectures there. When I returned to the sacristy after preaching, the pastor thanked me for what I had said. I was not a little surprised, because what I had said had been a hard saying. Pastor Harms later became Bishop of Oldenburg. After one visitation he said to the pastor whose work and preaching he had evaluated, "Pastor, you have withheld the gospel from your congregation." I esteem this bishop very highly for taking such a decisive stand against modern theology.

A pastor can lead his flock, his congregation to biblical pasturage, but he can also lead them into the desert, into barren places, astray.

To protect. It is impossible to speak about the office of shepherd without recalling the greatest shepherd of all: Jesus Christ, the Son of the living God. Similarly, it is impossible to discuss this theme without citing the great shepherd hymn, Psalm 23:

> The Lord is my shepherd; I shall not want.
> He maketh me to lie down in green pastures: he leadeth me beside the still waters.
> He restoreth my soul: he leadeth me in the paths of righteousness for his name's sake.
> Yea, though I walk through the valley of the shadow of death, I will fear no evil: for thou art with me; thy rod and thy staff they comfort me.
> Thou preparest a table before me in the presence of mine enemies: thou anointest my head with oil; my cup runneth over.
> Surely goodness and mercy shall follow me all the days of my life: and I will dwell in the house of the Lord for ever.

In this psalm, one statement is especially striking: "Thy rod and thy staff they comfort me." What is that supposed to mean?

This image derives from the period when the Near East was still infested with predatory animals that would break into the flock, attack some of the sheep, and kill them. For defense against these animals the shepherd had a heavy staff with a notch at the end. From the time they were very young, all the shepherd boys would practice putting rocks in these notches to hurl accurately at a target.

The shepherd's staff or rod was therefore reassuring to the sheep. It meant: the shepherd is there and will protect us.

Shepherds of souls, too, need means of protection against ravening wolves that break into the flock. Jesus warns about them in Matthew 7:15: "Beware of false prophets, which come to you in sheep's clothing, but inwardly they are ravening wolves."

Today in modern theology and in extreme movements there are many wolves in sheep's clothing, who throw the flocks into confusion with their peculiar doctrines. Therefore the Lord created the office of watchman to protect his flock. In Ezekiel 3:17, we read: "Son of man, I have made thee a watchman unto the house of Israel: therefore hear the word at my mouth, and give them warning from me."

True pastors, true shepherds, lead, provide, and protect.

22. Stewards (oikonomos) (I Peter 4:10)

In this text from Peter, the Greek original contains the phrase *oikonomos poikiles charitos theou*—stewards of the manifold grace of God."

It would be a rewarding task to write a theology of grace, a detailed discussion of the various manifestations of God's grace. In scholastic theology there was more reflection on grace than there is today. I can still recall vividly a lecture by Prof. Ruckert at the University of Tubingen on the scholastic doctrine of grace. Closest to the later teaching of the Reformers was *gratia gratis data*—grace that is given freely.

We have a God who overwhelms His children with His riches and makes them stewards of all He gives.

I have been to the Tower of London twice, where I have viewed the crown jewels of the English royal house. They are all under glass, where no one can touch them. Strong and effective precautionary measures have been taken to protect them. Guards stand close by to keep an eye on visitors. All one can do with these treasures is look at them. I had the same experience in the gold museum in Bogota (Columbia): mountains of gold and jewelry but you can only look at them.

The situation is different with our God. He puts these treasures in our very hands. We can claim them as our own. What are these treasures?

Jer. 31:14: Fulness of gifts

Ps. 16:11: Fulness of joy

Mal. 3:10: Fulness of blessings

John 1:16: Fulness of grace

Rom. 6:23: God's gift of eternal life

John 17:14: The gift of His Word

John 17:22: The gift of His glory

II Peter 1:4: The gift of great and precious promises

The series could go on and on. The only question is what we do with these gifts. The Lord distributes His riches, He entrusts us with His "pounds," for us to manage. We are appointed His stewards. Will we bury our share, as the unfaithful servant in Luke 19:11 did? Or will we set to work with what the Lord has entrusted to us?

We are responsible for what we undertake with our time, our strength, our money, and our property. We must give and accounting of our stewardship of the Word of God, of the promises of the Bible.

When we realize this clearly, then we must surrender our lives anew to the Lord, with everything He has entrusted to us.

I remember a woman who was very poorly dressed and lived in great poverty. I visited her at home twice. When she died and her will was read, her heirs were dumbfounded. She had some $480,000 in the bank. Think of what she could have done with it during her lifetime! At her own expense she could have supported two missionaries on the mission field. As it was, the state took a large chunk in the form of inheritance taxes. This woman can no longer make good in eternity what she failed to do with her great wealth while she was alive.

But we must not look down on this woman. Are we not equally irresponsible with the Word of the God and His promises?

Are we faithful stewards or unfaithful servants? Faithful management of everything entrusted to him by the Lord is expected of every Christian. Above and beyond this, there is also a talent and gift of stewardship that derives from the Holy Spirit.

Take, for example, the life of prayer. Every Christian must have times of prayer and a prayer life, otherwise he is not a Christian. But there are some of God's children who have a special priestly ministry of intercession and worship. I recall, for example, Mother Knies, the mother of the gospel singer Franz Knies. She devoted several hours, sometimes as many as seven or eight, to prayer each day. That cannot be imitated. In such a life we are dealing with an instance of special vocation, a very great grace and gift of the Spirit. It was faithful stewardship in using the biblical possibilities to the fullest. For her, every day was a "day of the open door" (Rev. 3:8: "Behold, I have set before thee an open door, and no man can shut it").

23. Speaking under the discipline and power of God (laein os logia theou) (I Peter 4:11)

A few years ago I was in Madeira for a brief visit. I was interested in the work of the fishermen as they came home with their catch each morning. I most enjoyed seeing the kinds of fish brought back by the deep-sea cutters. There were fish that I had never seen before, almost three feet long, black with several white stripes. I asked what they were called and where they were found. I could not understand the name in the Portugese jargon of the fishermen. The place where they were found therefore fascinated me all the more. They use reels of steel wire and special equipment to bring these fish up from a depth of 6,500 feet. The trouble is worth it, for the flesh of the fish is very tasty. I had been aware that Prof. Piccard, the deep sea explorer, had descended some 35,000 feet in the Philippine Trench. But catching fish at a depth of 6500 feet was something new to me.

This experience among the fishermen of Madeira suggested another image to me. If it were nothing more than an image, it would not be so bad. But it is a horrible reality.

There are believing fishermen who do the work of Satan. Or do they think what they are doing is at the behest of God? What is meant by all this?

In Micah 7:18-19 we read:

"Who is a God like unto thee, that pardoneth iniquity, and passeth by the transgression of the remnant of his heritage? he retaineth not his anger for ever, because he delighteth in *Mercy*.

"He will turn again, he will have compassion upon us; he will subdue our iniquities; and thou wilt cast all their sins into the *depths of the sea*."

Now what happens to all the sins that are cast by God's mercy into the depths of the sea?

There are pious fishermen who haul them up again and bring these sensational fish to the market-place, where everyone can see them, buy them, and take them home. How much suffering and agony is caused by these fishermen on both sides of the Atlantic! They think they are doing God a service by going fishing and then displaying their catch, thereby vitiating the work of another messenger of Jesus.

Some of the best known of their number, W. and S., said it had to be done to keep the gospel pure. As though mercy could adulterate the gospel—and legalism keep it pure! One of the most tragic examples took place in the fall of 1974. All the evangelically minded clergy of a Canadian city had planned a joint campaign with a missionary. During the period when preparations were being made, a certain Brother B. traveled to Canada from western Switzerland to visit his son. He reported a sensational incident in the recent life of the missionary who had been invited. The son quickly told the clergy. They held a meeting in which it was decided to cancel the services with the missionary. This took place in September 1974. The Swiss visitor returned home, where he relaxes in his comfortable suburban home. He did a good deed while he was abroad. At least that is his view.

A few years ago I was staying at the Hotel Bellevue in Switzerland for a rest. Among the many postcards and cards with Bible verses there was a card designed by Corrie ten Boom. The card has a picture of a broad sea. Above it stands a cross on which is inscribed Micah 7:18-19. At the bottom is a sign: NO FISHING. A truly original card, typical of Corrie. And she is right. But many pious fishermen ignore the sign.

"They shall put you out of the synagogues: yea, the time cometh, that whosoever killeth you will think that he doeth God service" (John 16:2)

This book about the gifts of the Spirit is written not for men of this world, but for believers. Therefore we are speaking here of the sins committed by the tongues of the devout, not of unbelievers.

The discourse of believers is limited by James 3:8 and I Peter 4:11:

"But the tongue can no man tame: it is an unruly evil, full of deadly poison";

"If any man speak, let him speak as the oracles of God."

Who can stand before this judgment? Jesus told His disciples:

"Every idle word that men shall speak, they shall give account thereof in the day of judgment" (Matt. 12:36).

Some alert readers will now want to admonish me in turn and say, "Look at the way you talked about your Western critics. Was that not devoid of love?"

Let me reply. When I receive letters in which I am personally insulted, they go at once into the wastebasket. I do not answer them, in private or in public. Whenever someone has reviled Jesus when He was on earth, He held His tongue. We, too, must hold our tongues, since we have ourselves offended thousands of times.

In the case of the false reports about Indonesia, however, we are dealing not only with a public problem but with a danger to the church of Jesus throughout the world. The articles of the Western critics, and above all the article "Indonesia Revival, True or False," have been reprinted by many missionary papers in every continent. What have the consequences been?

a. The church of Jesus has been robbed of the joy it had in the Indonesia revival.

b. The conviction of other critics and rationalists has been reinforced: the whole thing is a fraud.

c. The shadow of this criticism also falls on the other areas of revival. People say if the reports about Indonesia were wrong, we must also put the other revivals under the microscope.

d. This criticism had bad effects in turn on the Indonesian revival territory, as Pastor Daniel of Soe reported.

e. The negative tone of these articles has also caused those who had wonderful experiences with their Lord during the revival period to suffer a certain loss of courage. Many nationals have gone astray through the efforts of Western Christians.

f. A secondary effect of the dissemination of Western criticism has been a sharp drop in the sales of my book on Indonesia, as wholesalers on every continent have reported to me. This economic factor is the least important, although it amounts to thousands.

g. The primary point is that the devil has succeeded

in turning truth into lies and lies into truth. This technique of Satan will increase mightily as the end approaches.

It is easy for me to hold my tongue in the face of personal calumnies. In the face of this world-wide perversion of the facts, however, it is impossible to keep silent. The watchman's office, which the Lord has entrusted to His messengers, requires that they speak out. In this context, let us recall Acts 20:28-30, a passage already discussed:

"Take heed therefore unto yourselves, and to all the flock, over the which the Holy Spirit hath made you overseers, to feed the church of God, which he hath purchased with his own blood.

"For I know this, that after my departing shall grievous wolves enter in among you, not sparing the flock.

"Also of your own selves shall men arise, speaking perverse things, to draw away disciples after them."

Jesus said to His disciples: "For by thy words thou shalt be justified, and by thy words thou shalt be condemned" (Matt. 12:37)

Who among us can stand before the judgment of this criterion? Have we spoken like the oracles of God, *lalein os logia theou?*

The prophet Isaiah is familiar with this problem. He cried out:

"Woe is me! for I am undone; because I am a man of unclean lips, and I dwell in the midst of a people of unclean lips."(6:5)

But how full of comfort and hope are the following verses from Isaiah 6:6-7:

"Then flew one of the seraphims unto me, having

a live coal in his hand, which he had taken with the tongs from off the altar: And he laid it upon my mouth, and said, Lo, this hath touched thy lips; and thine iniquity is taken away, and thy sin purged'

Do we not all need to have our lips purged of sin? I know that I do.

What has been said to this point about the twenty-third gift of the Spirit has less to do with a gift of eloquence than with our mode of speech: speak under the discipline of God. In other words, we are dealing with the disciplining of our discourse, the discipline of the Holy Spirit. It is speech under the control and guidance of the Holy Spirit. This is a passive process. We are those who are ruled by the Holy Spirit.

There is naturally also an active side to the gift of eloquence: proclaiming the gospel with authority. It has already been pointed out that we are not speaking of the rhetoric that comes as a natural talent, but of "drawing strength from on high."

The Bible furnishes a good example. Think of the powerful words uttered by Elijah on Mount Carmel in I Kings 18, to which God responded with fire.

Think of the Sermon on the Mount. At its conclusion, those who were listening declared, "He taught them as one having authority" (Matt. 7:29).

Think of the death of Stephen, the first martyr. Luke records in Acts 7:54: "When they heard these things, they were cut to the heart, and they gnashed on him with their teeth."

In the Bible, in the history of the church and its mission, there are many who bear witness to Jesus with authority. Otto Siegfried von Bibra therefore entitled his well-known book *Men with Christ's Authority*.

Even the most brilliant and witty rhetoric without the Holy Spirit is mere empty words, which never lead to the life of the Spirit.

24. Certainty (pepeismai) (Rom. 8:38); (elegchos) (Heb. 11:1)

In Romans 8:38, the apostle Paul confesses:

"For I am persuaded, that neither death, nor life, nor angels, nor principalities, nor powers, nor things present, nor things to come, nor height, nor depth, nor any other creature, shall be able to separate us from the love of God, which is in Christ Jesus our Lord."

This certainty is not assurance of the flesh, grounded on our moral and religious qualities. Recall Matthew 7:22, where people come forward and recount to the eternal Judge their religious achievements, with which they hope to gain entrance into God's kingdom. There we read:

"Many will say to me in that day, Lord, Lord, have we not prophesied in thy name? and in thy name have cast out devils? and in thy name done many wonderful works?

"And then will I profess unto them, I never knew you: depart from me, ye that work iniquity."

According to this text, then, it is possible to prophesy, to cast out devils, to perform wonderful works, to speak in tongues, and much more—and still be cast out as an evildoer by Jesus.

This certainty is not the crazy notion of a paranoid or a religious neurotic. Many false prophets and

161

religious supermen are sowing discord and confusion today in the church of Jesus. They follow will-o'-the-wisps, products of their own confused fantasy, and carry others with them into the abyss.

This certainty is based on a rebirth brought about by the Holy Spirit. This certainty arises through the *testimonium spiritus sancti,* the testimony or witness of the Holy Spirit. Paul writes of it in Romans 8:16: "The Spirit itself beareth witness with our spirit, that we are the children of God." Here it is the Holy Spirit alone who is the agent, not the reborn Christian.

Several times in my life I have come in contact with the work of George Muller in Bristol, England. When he was ninety-three, this man of God bore witness: "For seventy-three years, ever since I was twenty and took Jesus as my Savior, I have never lost the certainty of salvation and of being a child of God."

To be a child of God does not mean to be sinless. We remain sinners to the end of our lives. But children of God have their offenses forgiven, and do not lose the gift with which the Holy Spirit has sealed them.

In Hebrews 11:1, certainty is also referred to as *elegchos ou blepomenon,* "evidence of things not seen." This process of being made certain is not rationally comprehensible. It is a mystery that cannot be understood, but only experienced.

We have come to end of our list of the twenty-four gifts. To repeat: the enumeration has no significance. Other exegetes will come up with other numbers.

Opinions can also differ about the order of the

gifts. Related gifts can be grouped together, as they are in Ephesians 4:11: apostles, prophets, evangelists, pastors, teachers. In this presentation, I wanted to follow the order of the text. We began with Corinthians. Then followed Romans, Ephesians, and Peter. The list concludes with Romans 8 and Hebrews 11.

We must not forget the gift above every gift: Jesus. He is not a gift of the Holy Spirit, but the gift of God. In Jesus the Father has opened to us once more the Paradise that had been lost. In Jesus He has given us eternal life, eternal salvation. This Jesus is the foundation and goal of our eternal life. In eternal glory stand only two thrones: that of God and that of the Lamb (Rev. 22:1). At the eschaton, the Holy Spirit will not have a throne. The function of the Holy Spirit is to glorify the Son of God (John 16:14). Therefore we will glorify Him at this point in the words of Revelation 4:10-11:

> "The four and twenty elders fall down before him that sat on the throne, and worship him that liveth for ever and ever, and cast their crowns before the throne, saying:
>
> "Thou art worthy, O Lord, to receive glory and honour and power: for thou hast created all things, and for thy pleasure they are and were created."

NOT TO SHAKE THE FOUNDATIONS

The religious movements of the present break

down into those that are extroverted, directed outward, and those that are introverted, directed inward.

The extroverted movements are unruly phenomena. Mass healing—ecstatic sects —spectacular assemblies.

Dancing—hand-clapping—rolling on the floor —these are all things I have not seen in Germany, but only in other countries. But they are phenomena like those that appeared in Germany in 1908 and 1909.

In the face of all these movements, we must insist; our church is a church of God's Word, not of ecstasy.

We must adhere firmly to the foundation rediscovered by the Reformers: *sola scriptura*, Holy Scripture alone. Our emotions, our experiences, however justified they may sometimes be, are not the basis for our life of faith, but rather it is the Holy Scripture.

The introverted movements, which tend to turn inward, are the meditation movements that have been publicized during the past few years in the Western world, primarily by people from India. Germany has been less affected than the United States and Canada.

Yogis introduce the various meditation exercises of Eastern Asia. Maharishis teach so-called transcendental meditation. For these exercises the adept, who is studying meditation, can choose himself a guru, a director. Buddha is often selected, but so are other religious leaders. Even Jesus can serve as a guru, though this does not mean that He is accepted as Son of God and redeemer. Meditation is a quiet affair. Among the educated, however, it is even more seductive than ecstatic confusion. Satan is wise, and knows how to appeal to everyone in his own way.

To these introverted disciples of meditation, we must say: *solus Christus,* Christ alone, but not as a guru, but as redeemer and Savior of all mankind, and our Lord.

The extroverted include the social activists. Love for one's neighbor, put into practice, lies within the framework of what the Bible requires. But this social activism preached today by the modernists is a counterfeit religion. Its followers build up the mosaic of their highway to heaven out of many little individual acts of charity. In the face of this errone- ous and misguided social consciousness, we must say: *sola gratia,* by grace alone.

"By grace are ye saved," Paul insists to the Ephesians (2:8). Redemption is not earned by social responsibility, but bestowed by God. After redemp- tion, the practical expression of love comes automat- ically.

It remains to mention the mystics. In New York I came across a group with mystical inclinations. Young people lie on their backs in front of the altar of a Catholic church. They spread out their arms at their sides to imitate the form of a cross. In this way they try to achieve an emotional rapport with the crucifixion. This brings them quite close to our clas- sic mystics like Eckhart, Suso, and Tauler, who as- pired to the *unio mystica,* mystical union with God. To those who are caught up in religious cult and devotional ceremony, we must say: *sola fide,* through faith alone. The bridge to God is not a feel- ing of devotion, but the faith by which we can grasp the salvation offered by God.

165

God's offer of salvation, Holy Scripture, contains all that we need for life and death. "Christ Jesus, who of God is made unto us wisdom, and righteousness, and sanctification, and redemption" (I Cor. 1:30). The Holy Spirit is the mediator of all this for us. He makes it real and actual. He makes it possible for us to appropriate salvation in *faith*.

PRAYER REQUESTS

During 1974 I had two lecture tours in the United States and one with my friend, Gottfried Amend in eastern Canada.

The North American continent is increasingly overrun by heretical movements and satanic cults. One man who knows America well said: "The land where the Pilgrim fathers landed in 1620 with much prayer seems today to be sinking in a sea of demonism."

This situation is the reason behind most of my invitations to lecture. And how I often fear these tours! I am constantly requested to speak about occultism and give some guidance for pastoral work.

I continue to need serious intercession. My work of enlightenment and pastoral counseling in the realm of the occult is a battle with the powers of darkness. They counterattack furiously. I wish the Lord had chosen Himself another instrument for this work. I am nearly broken by these struggles.

At times, however, the Lord gives strong encouragement for this difficult service. I have already told about the conversion of Ives Petelle, the young astrologer from Quebec. I ask once more that the believing readers of this book pray for him.

Another experience gave me renewed courage. I was already correcting the proofs for this book when I received news from East Germany. The leader of a spiritualist sect that has some six thousand members scattered throughout Saxony sent me greetings through an intermediary. I must keep his name secret, because otherwise I would be exposing this man to danger.

It was some years ago that a believing Christian gave this spiritualist leader some of my books written in opposition to occultism. He read these books, and became uneasy and insecure in his mediumistic practices. A few years later he received a tape with a lecture on deliverance from possession. (I do not have a single tape myself, so please do not request any tapes from me.) In this lecture I cited an example that made an impact on the spiritualist. He said to himself, "That's the same thing we have in our circles." Now he could have no inner peace. A believing brother crossed the path of this spiritualist. After a terrible struggle, this leading spiritualist was set free and surrendered his life to Jesus, along with sixty others. Today he is licensed to preach in East

Germany, and delivers lectures against his former sect. He is a great help to the pastors and their congregations. Now, while this book was being published, this brother thanked me for the help he had found through my books and the tape. It is not to my credit that such things happen. All help comes from the Lord and not from us, His unworthy witnesses.

The necessity for intercession is also illustrated by an unfortuate experience. Last year I bought a new car. When I was invited to come to a city in northern Germany to speak about *The Exorcist* and satanic cults, I had a strange automobile accident, the outcome of which was total destruction of my car and three broken ribs for me. A forest worker wanted to make a left turn onto a trail and cut me off. The police told me: "It's a miracle that you got out of this wreck alive." Satan wanted to thwart this series of lectures, but the Lord intervened. All evangelists and messengers of Jesus, from Wesley, Moody, Blumhardt, and Johannes Seitz down to the present day, know the powers of darkness counterattack when one seeks to unmask them.

Very often I hear Christians quote I John 4:4: "Greater is he that is in you, than he that is in the world." These brethren sometimes think the devil cannot harm believers. I agree strongly with this text, but in spite of it I know of the heavy attacks of Satan. Let me give you some examples.

In 1969 two missionaries of the Regions Beyond Mission went into the inner part of New Guinea, where they were killed and eaten by cannibals. Did Satan touch them or not?

In 1974 in the neighborhood of Djajapura (formerly Hollandia), New Guinea pagans attacked a Christian congregation. They killed fourteen Christians and ate them. Did Satan touch these believers or not? Of course, only their bodies were destroyed—not their souls.

In 1975, on my thirty-third preaching tour in the USA, I had a counseling session in California with a former satanist. He gave me permission to publish his story in order to gain the help of prayer warriors. I will give only a short report on this person, who is a high school teacher.

One night he heard a satanist on a TV program. The satanist declared: "All religious sources have failed. Whoever desires power must deliver his life over to Satan." What a terrible thing that devil worshipers are allowed to appear on the screen in some countries!

So this teacher gave his life over to Satan. His wife and his mother-in-law (both earnest Christians) prayed much for him and gave him my books *Between Christ and Satan* and *Occult Bondage and Deliverance*. The living God performed a miracle. The teacher became willing to stop worshipping the devil. He started to pray and finally gave his life to the Lord. In a short time he became strong in his testimony, and went back to the place where the satanists used to practice the black mass and devil worship. It was the "skeleton canyon" near Thousand Oaks, California, between Los Angeles and Santa Barbara. He witnessed for Christ from four o'clock until midnight, and won a number of satanists for the Lord.

But now the devil appeared to him and threatened: "If you do not come back to me, I will kill your child and ruin you financially." At this time his child was healthy, but the next morning he suddenly fell ill and was taken to the hospital. Three weeks later he died, and the hospital bill came to $13,000. Satan literally fulfilled his terrible promise. I ask you, did the devil touch this believer or not? The problem is not as easy as superficial Christians think.

This high school teacher had to undergo satanic attacks without the support of a strong prayer group. Most of his fellow Christians didn't wish to have anything to do with him. Some even thought he should go to a psychiatric clinic. It is an unbelievable situation that Christians do not know how to stand the battle in such a case and are not able to help such a brother. It is for this reason that I tell this story and ask all Christians who have a solid prayer life to intercede for this one who is in the battleline against the powers of darkness. He has already given his testimony in many churches and proclaims the victory of Jesus over all satanic power.

Just before the proofsheets were returned to the typesetters I received a letter from South Africa dated June, 1975. The General Manager of a Christian literature centre gave me the following report: "I am at the present time reading your book *Between Christ and Satan*. It has been a tremendous blessing to me. Once again I realize the great importance and necessity in getting these books out to Christians.

"We have just recently lost our little 4½ year old boy very tragically. We were on our way to Pretoria to have dealings with the Department of Prisons to place libraries into prisons. The Department had given authority to the Christian literature center to place such libraries into every prison in South Africa. We arrived on Friday night and the next morning our little boy drowned. After this drowning our little 2½ year old daughter was tortured by an evil spirit. We brought her to an evangelist. After praying together, the evangelist in the name of Jesus commanded the evil forces and God stepped in immediately.

"In reading your books we see that the enemy is literally a roaring lion seeking whom he may devour."

I abbreviated the report because the letter is too long for this book. You see here the same workings of the archenemy. This active brother in South Africa was going to start a wonderful work in the prisons. Therefore Satan tried to hinder and discourage him by haunting his family. He had the same experience which I had for years when I was preaching, teaching and lecturing throughout the continents.

In spite of all — Jesus is Victor!

Let me conclude with the tremendous promise of our Lord given in Luke 10:19: "Behold, I give unto you power to tread on serpents and scorpions, and over all the power of the enemy: and nothing shall by any means hurt you." Though Satan is a mighty enemy—one who is able to attack believers—Christ is an almighty friend who has the last word against the powers of darkness.

OTHER WORKS BY THE AUTHOR

In his German language Dr. Kurt E. Koch has written over 70 titles which have now more than 60 foreign translations. These include English, French, Spanish, Portuguese, Danish, Norwegian, Swedish, Finnish, Japanese, Korean, Polish, Afrikaans, Hungarian, Italian, and yet more. Some appeared under a pseudonym.

Only the languages which are spoken in North America are mentioned below.

Kregel Publications, P.O. Box 2607, Grand Rapids, MI 49501 has 14 titles in English.

Between Christ and Satan
Charismatic Gifts
Christian Counseling and Occultism
Day X
Demonism, Past and Present
Devil's Alphabet
Occult Bondage and Deliverance
Revival Fires in Canada
Strife of Tongues
The Coming One
The Revival in Indonesia
The Wine of God
Victory Through Persecution (The Korean Revival)
World Without Chance?

The Association for Christian Evangelism (Quebec) Inc., 747, 81st Avenue, Chomedey-Level (Montreal) Quebec, Canada has 8 titles in French:

Occultisme et cure d'ame (Christian Counselling and Occultism)
Le Jour "X" (Day "X")
Le réveil de Timor
Quand les Coréens prient (Victory through Persecution)
Puissance plus grande que la dynamite
Esclavage occulte et délivrance (Occult Bondage and Deliverance)
Entre Christ et Satan (Between Christ and Satan)
Le conflit des langues (The Strife of Tongues)

Editorial Clie; Moragas Barret, 113; Tarrasa (Barcelona), Spain. Office in U.S.A. - Box 6094, Grand Rapids, MI 49506 has 3 titles in Spanish:

Ocultismo y cura de almas (Christian Counselling and Occultism)
Entre Cristo y Satanás (Between Christ and Satan)
El diccionario del Diablo (The Devil's Alphabet)

Distributors of Books by Kurt E. Koch:
U.S.A.: Kregel Publications, P.O. Box 2607, Grand Rapids,
MI 49501

Canada: Home Evangel Books, 565 Gordon Baker Rd.,
Willowdale, Ontario, Canada, M2H 2W2

England: Marshall, Morgan and Scott, 116 Baker Rd.,
London WIM, 2BB

South Africa: Word of Life Wholesale, P.O. Box 698, Florida,
Transvaal

New Zealand: G.W. Moore, Ltd., 24 Empire Road, Epsom,
Auckland, Box 29012

Australia: S. John Bacon Publishing, 12-13 Windsor Ave.
Mr. Waverley, Victoria

Switzerland: Brunnen Verlag, Spalenberg 20, CH 4001 Basel